Praise for *The Changeover Zone*

"I love how the change in a church pastor is seen not as an event but as a process and from various key perspectives. This will be a valuable tool for my coaching with pastors and churches who are entering a season of transition."
—Ken Willard, leadership coach, certified church consultant, and author, *Time Management for the Christian Leader*

"When our church learned that both long-tenured pastors were leaving at the same, we knew we needed expert help. Jim Ozier led our leaders in a workshop based on *The Changeover Zone* to prepare us for this scary change. In this book the authors use sound biblical footing to show you what to do and how to do it as you go through a pastoral change."
—Cheryl Lee, SPPR Chairman, Ebenezer United Methodist Church, Suffolk, VA

"As a pastor following a long-tenured founding pastor, I implemented the authors' simple yet brilliant applications, and my transition into this role has been strikingly effortless. Following their step-by-step guide, the congregation was incorporated into the process early, so by the time I arrived the congregation and I felt as if we had known each other for quite some time. This has led to immediate buy-in, and in nine month's time we are seeing incredible growth."
—Tim Jones, pastor, Sycamore Tree United Methodist Church

"The action plan for the one hundred days before and after a change of pastors (the Changeover Zone) is brimming with time-tested wisdom. Pastors, churches, and supervisors will be prepared to not only minimize the pain and confusion that comes with pastoral transitions but actually maximize the potential for growth and new life in congregations."
—Ken Irby, Shreveport District Superintendent, Louisiana Annual Conference, United Methodist Church

"I have been using the authors' advice on making a great handoff for years. You will nod your head as you read, and say, *Of Course*. Keep nodding. It will make a difference in raising up stronger leaders and building reproducible systems."
—Cathy Townley, Townley Coaching

"The sacred mission of the church is passed from person to person, generation to generation. *The Changeover Zone* captures the essence of the spirit with which clergy and laity must approach pastoral transitions."
—Stacey Piyakhun, pastor, Melissa United Methodist Church, Melissa, TX

"When a pastoral change happens, there are many questions being asked as part of the grief and transition process. *The Changeover Zone* anticipates these questions, helping leaders answer critical inquires even before they are asked."
—Phil Schroeder, Director of Congregational Development, North Georgia Conference (UMC)

Also from Author Jim Ozier

Clip In: Risking Hospitality in Your Church

Other Recommended Titles from Abingdon Press

*Time Management for the Christian Leade*r by Ken Willard

The
CHANGE
OVER
ZONE

Successful Pastoral Transitions

Jim Ozier & Jim Griffith

Abingdon Press
Nashville

THE CHANGEOVER ZONE:
SUCCESSFUL PASTORAL TRANSITIONS

Copyright © 2016 by Abingdon Press

All rights reserved.

Library of Congress Cataloging-in-Publication Data

Names: Ozier, Jim, author.
Title: The changeover zone : successful pastoral transitions / Jim Ozier &
   Jim Griffith.
Description: Nashville : Abingdon Press, 2016.
Identifiers: LCCN 2016009067 | ISBN 9781501810411 (pbk.)
Subjects: LCSH: Clergy--Relocation. | Church management. | Organizational
   change--Management. | Change--Religious aspects--Christianity.
Classification: LCC BV664 .O95 2016 | DDC 253/.2--dc23 LC record available at http://
lccn.loc.gov/2016009067

Scripture quotations unless noted otherwise are from the Common English Bible. Copyright © 2011 by the Common English Bible. All rights reserved. Used by permission. www.CommonEnglishBible.com.

Scripture quotations marked NRSV are taken from the New Revised Standard Version of the Bible, copyright 1989, Division of Christian Education of the National Council of the Churches of Christ in the United States of America. Used by permission. All rights reserved.

The Successful Second Pastors Study on page 119–25 is reprinted with permission from the Lewis Center for Church Leadership of Wesley Theological Seminary, Washington, DC, www.churchleadership.com.

16 17 18 19 20 21 22 23 24 25—10 9 8 7 6 5 4 3 2 1
MANUFACTURED IN THE UNITED STATES OF AMERICA

CONTENTS

v

SECTION THREE: Following the Long-Tenured Pastor

Passing the Baton in the Changeover Zone

*History tells sad stories of good churches
that are calcified as monuments to former pastors.*

—Colin Hansen

When is the right time to begin thinking about pastoral transition? From day one, when a pastor first begins her or his tenure as the pastor of a local church! While the life of a local church may well be seen in terms of a long marathon, the pastoral leadership—regardless of how long any one pastor serves a particular church—is best seen as a relay race, in which the current pastor prepares to pass the baton on to a successor in that crucial segment of time and space called *the changeover zone.* That is why Bruce Miller says, "Pastoring a church is not getting a trophy to keep; it is getting a baton to pass."

Biblical history is a testimony to leaders of God's people moving through changeover zones, passing their batons to successors. Whether it was Elijah passing the mantel to Elisha or Moses giving way to Joshua, wise leaders know their leadership won't last forever, nor should it. Belief that ministry is a journey into God's future compels us to pass the baton in a way that makes possible even more success under the leadership of the successor.

When Jesus handed off the baton to Peter, it was with an ultimately victorious church in mind. When pastors—from day one—begin to pray for and prepare their successor, it does not lead (as supervisors sometimes fear) to shortsightedness, or lack of total commitment. Rather, it leads to a cultural mindset that, as the pastor, one of my main jobs is to prepare the church to do even greater ministry when my successor arrives.

Pastoral leadership is a relay race. In The United Methodist Church, bishops and cabinets invest long hours and a lot of emotional energy to match a church and its mission field's needs with the right pastor. They pray about, agonize over, and deliberate on how to successfully make appointments. Ironically, the time demands and myriad duties of district superintendents allow them far less time to make the appointment successful.

It is our hope that this book will help streamline and provide some tools to improve the transition process—in short, to pass the baton in a smooth, seamless transition that allows the successor to get off to a running start.

We have written this book from a wealth of experience in helping churches in pastoral transitions: Jim Ozier, in addition to coaching, consulting, and conducting workshops in more than thirty annual conferences of The United Methodist Church, also has served on the Appointive Cabinet of the North Texas Conference for seven years. Jim Griffith has worked with hundreds of churches and a multitude of tribal judicatories and independent churches and nondenominational churches for over twenty years.

This book takes the experience we've learned from dozens of transition situations and distills our learnings into best practices for pastors, supervisors, and churches when it comes to passing the baton. It will help you create a culture and common language to plan and execute a successful transition; it will help you avoid the many pitfalls and mistakes that derail a new pastor from getting off to a running start. More important, we'll share how to do pastoral transitions that go beyond "surviving it" to actually accelerate growth during the transition!

The Changeover Zone is where carefully thought-out, prepared-for, practiced roles come together with remarkable results. This book explores every role involved with a pastoral transition in the Changeover Zone of ministry:

- what supervisors and judicatory leaders can do to ensure a smooth handoff
- what the exiting founder can do to prepare to pass the baton
- what the new pastor can do to seamlessly receive the baton
- what the church must do so their new pastor gets off to a running start

Perhaps you are that new pastor or the exiting founder. Perhaps you are in a supervisory role or are a member of the church going through its first pastoral change. Whatever part you may be playing in the transition, this book can serve as a step-by-step guide to a successful transition and a smooth handoff. This is a momentous—and often fragile—time in a young congregation's life.

But this book is not just for new churches going through their first pastoral transitions. Many of the supervisors, congregations, and pastors we work with tell us that the principles we teach in new-church settings are applicable to all sorts of pastoral transitions. So the first section lays the foundation by dealing with pastoral transitions of any type; section two focuses on specific ways to apply these principles to new churches going through their first pastoral transition; and section three shows how and why to implement these techniques to transitions in long-tenured pastorates. In short, section one tells what to do; sections two and three show how to do it.

Why this book now? Because we want to help churches prepare for the unprecedented rise in pastoral retirements on the horizon.[1] This book hopes to help the church navigate through the great changes and changeovers coming our way. We have experienced first-hand from participants in our workshops, Following the Founder: Becoming a Successful Second Pastor, the pain, confusion, and frustration of pastors and churches going through poorly planned pastoral transitions.

This book is a response to what we have come to believe is a crying need of the church today. As you read it alone or with a transition team, you will discover specific techniques and practices that will be instrumental in getting transitions right when a church enters into the Changeover Zone.

Improving Pastoral Transitions

Chapter 1

Pastoral Leadership Is a Relay Race

Leadership is more like a baton than a trophy. You lift a trophy, but you hand off a baton.

—Bruce Miller, *The Leadership Baton*

I remember my first track meet like it was yesterday. Growing up in rural Illinois I was blessed with speed—lots of folks said I was "the fastest kid in Sangamon County." I was even more blessed to be invited by our junior high track coach to join the team. I admired my uniform, much too big for me but I didn't care. I was small, but I knew the speed I possessed and was confident. I looked down at my new cleats, excited and nervous about the race. In the lane to my left was the team from Illiopolis, the strong favorite, but the boys from Chatham on my right were just about as good. I knew nothing about the fourth team from Pleasant Plains, but it didn't really matter. I was fast. I knew I could beat all comers. Because of my sprinter's speed, I was chosen as a last-minute addition to the relay team. Coach had told me what I was supposed to do and I was ready to do it.

As I was sorting through all his instructions bouncing around in my brain, I couldn't wait for my teammate, Roger, to round the track on his leg of the race and hand off the baton to me. I heard his footsteps in the cinders. I was confident. I knew the drill: I looked behind me to the location next to the track where we had placed our marker. When my teammate Roger reached that spot I was supposed to spring from my starting position, accelerating into a sprint while I reached behind me, hand open, thumb down. Because Roger would already have momentum, he would catch up to me quickly, extending the baton forward, lunging toward the moment when we would actually exchange the baton. I would feel the slap of it into my hand and for a brief second we would run in tandem, his hand and mine both clinging to the baton. Slowly he would let go and fade back, and I would charge forward for the final victorious sprint of the race!

At least, that's what I was supposed to do. I didn't.

Instead, I panicked. I couldn't remember if I was supposed to slow down and let Roger catch up to me or if I was supposed to speed up. It all became jumbled: Was I supposed to extend my hand behind me or simply to my side? Palm up or palm down? I heard Roger shout, "Stick! Stick! Stick!" which is what he was coached to yell when it was time for me take the baton—but honestly, it sounded a lot like, "Stop! Stop! Stop!"

So that's what I did.

Roger's momentum carried him past me as he tried to find my hand. I did grab the baton for a split second, right before I dropped it. By the time I picked it up, sped past Roger who was partially clogging my lane, and found my stride, I was too far behind to catch up, even with my blazing speed.

After the race, I remember clutching the purple "Good Sportsmanship" ribbon as Coach walked us toward the locker room. He took the blame for inserting a new guy into the relay team, messing up its precision. At the same time he emphasized over and over to us all: "How fast you run will keep you in the race; how well you hand off will win it!"

While I didn't know it at the time, Coach Casey was teaching me one of the guiding principles of my future ministry: no matter how long the race, it's the handoff that is most important.

This book focuses primarily on that section of the pastoral transition, which happens just before and after the handoff from one pastor to another. This handoff occurs in what most track coaches refer to as the Changeover Zone.

It seeks to answer the question facing pastors and churches undergoing a transition: what are the tactics and strategies and behaviors essential to a good handoff in the Changeover Zone?

Success in the Changeover Zone

The race is about the baton, not the runners. The baton must always remain the fastest member of the squad.

—Coach Nigel Hetherinton

Casual fans of relay racing might mistakenly conclude that passing the baton is a single event that happens when one runner slaps the baton into the hand of another runner. But there is far more to it than that. In a relay race the critical moments happen in those twenty meters known as the changeover zone, where the hand off occurs, where a fast-paced series of events occurs seamlessly and results in a successful passing of the baton. Relay racers know that their success depends on a smooth, seamless hand off. It is not simply a matter of having fast athletes; all teams possess fast runners.

Beyond that, everyone on the team must know their roles, prepare for them, and be ready to execute them when the "incoming" runner moves into the changeover zone to hand off the baton to the "outgoing" runner. Teams that carefully prepare make seamless handoffs and position themselves for success; ones that don't prepare fumble the baton and no amount of natural skills can overcome the resulting failures. Coaches drill into their runners: "Get the most acceleration out of your zone! Exchange the baton at your top speed!" Great coaches with great teams know that to be successful you absolutely must have a smooth and seamless handoff. But a winning team does more than just the basics; it excels at accelerating out of the zone at top speed.

Within a mere twenty meters, both the incoming and outgoing runners are sprinting in tandem as the baton is passed. They blaze into an amazing high-speed, fast-paced ritual. The outgoing runner has been watching the race play out around the track, preparing mentally, jumping up and down to stay loose, positioning, watching, and listening for the "go, go, go" from the incoming runner.

Responding, the outgoing runner moves into place and launches into a sprint at precisely the time the incoming runner enters the changeover zone, listening for the words: "Stick! Stick! Stick!" On cue, the outgoing runner, running forward with arm extended back, receives the baton and accelerates through and out of the changeover zone.

A successful and seamless transition!

The Changeover Zone for a pastoral transition is similar. It's a length of time in which a precise set of activities take place, often at fast-paced frenetic speed, in which an amazing display of teamwork can make for a successful handoff of leadership responsibilities, and where the new pastor gets off to a running start.

Whatever the length of an actual pastoral transition, what happens during the Changeover Zone makes up the period of time in which the various participants—the pastors, church and leaders, and supervisors— execute a set of actions that have been thought out in advance (with the skills and strengths of the participants in mind), planned and prepared for, and carried out with the precision of a successful team.

Whether or not it is a planned succession, or more often, planning for a succession, every pastoral transition ends up becoming an example of passing the baton. It can be a glowing example of how to do it right or it can be a glaring example of how to do it wrong. But it becomes an example that helps set the culture of transition within any organization. So it is critical that supervisors/judicatories/pulpit committees evaluate their tactics in the Changeover Zone; whether seamless handoffs or botched ones, much can be learned and applied to future transitions.

Church culture is often revealed in words and attitudes. Note the difference when parishioners say, "We're going through a pastoral transition," as opposed to, "We're ready to charge into a time of pastoral transition!" Each statement refers to the same experience but reflects a totally different outlook. The first reflects a passive and resigned response, an unplanned event thrust upon the church, in some way of making it the victim, "Hang in there; we'll get through it." The latter response reflects a well-thought-out, predictable series of events, belying a confidence of enthusiasm, energy, and optimism that, regardless of the reasons for or timing of the pastoral change, conveys "Bring it on. This is a great opportunity for us!"

If pastors and churches are to get better at passing the baton, certainly a change of cultural mindset is required and it begins with the focused work of an entire team and what transpires in the Changeover Zone.

Since culture travels on words, the metaphors of "changeover zone" and "handoff" illustrate the various issues of pastoral transitions and communicating behaviors that lead to success in the Changeover Zone.

Chapter 2

The Changeover Zone in the Bible

I laid a foundation... but someone else is building on top of it.
—1 Corinthians 3:10 CEB

Charles Harper, the mayor of Wichita Falls, Texas, tells this story: When Charles graduated from college his father pulled him aside from the family celebration for a personal father-son moment. Ceremoniously he presented Charles with the "family axe." "Son," his father said, "this is the family axe. This is the same axe my father gave me when I became a man; it is the same axe his father gave to him; and his father gave your great-great-grandfather. This is the very axe that was used to clear this land when we homesteaded here in Wichita Falls."

Charles, just graduated from college, was full of vinegar and skepticism. "You mean to tell me, Dad, that this is the very same axe my great-great-great-grandfather used to clear this land?"

Wisely, his father answered, "Well, son, over the years it has had a few different heads and a few different handles, but it is the same axe."

So it is with the kind of tradition that bears deep meaning and focuses identity. At the risk of mixing metaphors, the story of this family axe partly explains the stories found in the Bible of the baton that is passed from one leader to the next: king to king, leader to leader, pastor to pastor, each period of time recounting a historic handoff.

"Appoint someone over the community...so that the LORD's community won't be like sheep without a shepherd" (Num 27:15-17 CEB). Sounds like a pastor doesn't it? Actually these are powerful words from Moses pleading with God to set up a leadership transition plan whose Changeover Zone required three books of the Old Testament—Numbers, Deuteronomy, and Joshua—to detail the story of a handoff.

First of all, Moses acknowledges the reason for the handoff: "I'm 120 years old today. I can't move around well anymore" (Deut 31:2 CEB) and in so doing steps into the Changeover Zone with Joshua, his appointed successor. The reasons for a pastoral change vary greatly; they include but are not limited to: death of a pastor, retirement, mismatched pastoral situation, unhealthy churches, underperforming pastor or church, changing times, changing demographics, pastor feeling called to another situation, timing, tenure, and on and on. But whatever the reason, acknowledging it as openly and as graciously as possible is essential to build and maintain trust. Trust is the key ingredient in the relational integrity that is so critical in the Changeover Zone. Runners in the relay race trust their teammates and coaches, which enhances performance and increases the likelihood of success.

Second, to increase the odds of a smooth, seamless transition, it is important for the congregation to see their departing pastor enthusiastically and publicly endorsing the successor. Notice the pattern in Numbers 27: Moses is told in verse 18 to "lay your hand on him [Joshua]," and then in verse 19, "Place him before Eleazar the priest and the entire community and commission him before them." And in verse 20, "You will give him some of your power so that the entire Israelite community may obey" (CEB).

Third, for a smooth and seamless transition, the incoming pastor must confidently accept the baton and lead. Immediately! In Joshua we see God blessing the transfer of leadership as well as the promise of his presence with the leader: "I will be with you in the same way I was with Moses. . . . I've commanded you to be brave and strong, haven't I? Don't be alarmed or terrified, because the LORD your God is with you wherever you go" (Josh 1:5; 9 CEB). In any transition, there will be tough times and difficult obstacles, but confidence in the ministry of the church is essential for the successor.

Accepting the baton to complete a smooth and seamless transition is possible when the successor truly seeks and sees God's hand in the transition and in the life of the church.

The Bible has many such stories of passing the baton. Because there are so many stories, there is no "one right way," rather a myriad of examples to consider. However, according to this passage, any candidate seeking to receive the baton has experienced and is living out a "call to ministry" as evidenced by the spirit of God and that spirit of God is within them. "The LORD said to Moses, 'Take Joshua, Nun's son, a man who has the spirit, and lay your hand on him'" (Num 27:18 CEB). Notice it seems to be a given that Joshua is a "man who has the spirit."

This call doesn't happen alone; it happens in the context of a community called to discern and assess the suitability of placement to a *particular ministry situation*. In verse 21 is that interesting phrase, "He will stand before Eleazar the priest, who will determine for him" (CEB).

It is imperative that judicatories have a prequalified pool of trained pastors to become second pastors following a founder and equally important to have trained pastors to follow long-term pastorates.

Based on the numerous biblical references to the Changeover Zone, all pastors should become students of these exchanges and the wisdom afforded. In another famous biblical transition, King David hands off leadership to Solomon. David had done great things: moved the capital to Jerusalem, restored the ark of the covenant, and began plans for a new temple.

These challenges provided a great legacy for David. However, they present a daunting task for Solomon. In David's own words: "My son Solomon, the one whom God chose, is too inexperienced for this great task" (1 Chron 29:1 CEB). So David did all he could to make the transition smooth, providing everything for the house of God as he was able.

Solomon made David's dream of the temple actually happen. As scripture reports so clearly, "Thus Solomon sat on the LORD's throne as king, succeeding his father David, and he prospered" (1 Chron 29:23 CEB).

In the next decade many pastors will retire and give way to younger, less experienced ones. God told Joshua then, "My servant Moses is dead. Now get ready to cross over the Jordan" (Josh 1:2 CEB). Just as important today, when transitions occur, God has ordained that leaders prepare themselves to step up and continue the mission of the Lord. Being ready, trained, and equipped for the transfer of leadership is paramount for the fruitfulness of God's church today.

Whether it is Elijah passing the mantle to Elisha (1 Kings 19:15-21) or Paul handing off leadership to young Timothy (1 Tim 4:11-16) or the disciples casting lots as a way to select the successor to Judas (Acts 1:12-25), the Bible records numerous instances of leadership transition. In each situation the baton is passed differently but passed nonetheless. One thing stands out: throughout redemptive history, passing the baton is one of the most critical elements of the entire biblical story, which elevates "passing the baton" to a high priority in churches facing a pastoral change.

Both Old and New Testament alike witness to the necessity of passing the baton. The baton is almost mystical or metaphysical. The baton is more important than either runner: it belongs to the church, but it is even more important than the local church. If the baton is simply seen as the reigns of leadership or the keeper of the flock, it will be seen administratively or in a corporate mindset. The baton must be seen as the sacred tradition that goes beyond any local church. It is the kingdom dimension made manifest *in* the local church. It embodies leadership but is not confined to it; it carries with it the responsibility of running the church, but there is more to it than that; it includes supervisory authority of pastoral oversight and maintaining the order of the church, but it goes deeper than that. More glorious than words can capture, it brings to life the word of God. The baton signifies that mysterious "It" handed down from generation to generation, beginning when Jesus birthed the church and destined to continue into God's future.

Pastoral leadership is a relay race, but it's all about the baton. It is the ever-present biblical mandate in the church. More than the pastors, more than the supervisors, even more than the congregation involved in the transition, it is all about the baton!

It means that the Changeover Zone should be viewed with humility and reverence and demands holy attention be given to the handoff to pass the baton in the most intentional way possible. And not just in a way that the church "gets through it." But rather in a way that creates excitement and accelerates the growth of the church *during* the transition.

Some have suggested that the modern-day, hollow baton currently used in relay races includes a military history—that messages were stuffed inside the baton and runners carried them from one battle site to another. If this tradition is true, it fits well into the handoff metaphor. Perhaps when we say, "It's all about the baton," we can remember that it holds within it the timeless message of God's salvation through Jesus Christ.

Chapter 3

The Role of Supervisors

Managing the Process

Ability is what you are capable of doing. Motivation determines what you do. Attitude determines how well you do it.

—Lou Holtz

Lifeway Research calculates that the average tenure of a pastor of any denomination or group is currently 3.6 years.[1] For supervisors and judicatories of churches, as well as the traditional pulpit committee, this is a daunting reminder that the bar has been raised for managing a good handoff, enabling the new incoming pastor and the church to get off to a good running start right from the beginning! The supervisor is the "on-the-field" manager of the Changeover Zone transition process. Many supervisors face the unfamiliar task of attempting to carry it out while managing other aspects of ministry/church life. Even more daunting, due to limited experience in the Changeover Zone, some supervisors may not understand their role, or appreciate the nuances sufficiently to ensure a smooth handoff.

Supervisors should bring a checklist of the five key functions in the Changeover Zone, listed below, and would do well to familiarize themselves with the sequence that occurs in the Changeover Zone. Skip or short-circuit even one and the transition is in peril:

1. Preparing
2. Positioning
3. Promoting
4. Preventing
5. Propelling

11

Preparing

In a relay race, the coach takes time to evaluate the demands of the race—distance, conditions, direction of wind, and so forth—and match each runner's strengths, weaknesses, even personality, to ensure proper placement in the rotation. Similarly, the clearer a supervisor can be about the transition needs—the personnel involved, the contextual needs of the church—the greater the chances of a smooth handoff. To help gain clarity about the specific needs and dynamics of any given transition, consider these preparation questions: What is the *strategy* needed? What are the *tactics* required?

Preparing is essential for supervisors to develop the right strategy for a particular transition, and to be able to communicate that strategy in a common language understood by all the principles: the supervisor, the departing pastor, the incoming pastor, and the local church. Remember, supervisors generally know their roles and try their best to carry them out with diligence, so the purpose of this chapter is to inform the other participants—the church leadership, the departing pastor, and the incoming pastor—what to *expect* from the supervisor of the transition.

Preparing must include healthy, well-thought-out profiling of the church and its current context. Profiling is not a negative thing; it does not mean stereotyping. Rather, the strategic thrust of the Changeover Zone begins with the supervisors having a clear grasp of what *kind of church* is going through a transition and being able to talk about it using a common language. In other words, "preparing the church." Remember, the idea here is not to become a brilliant or academic analyst of local churches but to develop a common language with which to assist local churches as supervisors. Without a common language all entities—supervisor, departing and incoming pastors, and church leadership—run the risk of talking over each other's heads, leading to unnecessary confusion and misunderstanding…and a botched handoff. Far too often, supervisors describe a particular church one way, the pastor of that church speaks about it another way, and the church leadership talks about it in yet a different way. No wonder it's hard to gain traction, solve problems, and develop fruitful ministries!

If the supervisors, pastors, and church leadership are not in agreement about the broad description that characterizes the church, the road forward will be filled with potholes and perils. Lack of consensus may lead to embracing a strategy and employing tactics that do not match the situation, causing frustration, disappointment, and unfulfilled expectations. So here are three possible tools we suggest that judicatories consider as ways to develop a common language. Select the option(s) that might best be utilized in your specific area.

The Life Context of the Church

One good approach is to adapt Michael Watkins's STARS profile, detailed in his classic leadership book *The First 90 Days*, which can effectively be adapted to the church culture and communication to help supervisors lead in transitions.[1] Using the common language, the supervisors, pastor, staff, and church should be able to agree that the church going through a transition is best characterized as a:

S=Startup—This is the easiest to identify as a new church or worshipping community, but where is it in terms of age and viability? A seven-month-old "new church" is dramatically different than a seven-year-old "new church" about to receive its first "new pastor." (Covered extensively in Section Two of this book.)

T=Turnaround—Every judicatory has once-strong churches who have declined numerically due to changing demographics, diminished intensity, or toxic situations. The decline may have been gradual over the years or more precipitous, but if it doesn't "turn around" it has little chance of a long-term future. This is also relatively easy to identify because the needs are so glaring and the morale of the church is usually sagging. Frequently a majority of the leadership and influencers no longer live in the neighborhood; the church is so swamped by mounting problems that it has little energy to find or focus on a vision.

A=Accelerated Growth—This is a church that has experienced a growth spurt and received lots of affirmation for it. However, the fast growth, rarely sustainable, has now slowed significantly even to the point of leveling off. Sudden growth spurts raise expectations that they will continue long term; sadly, they rarely do. This kind of church is much harder to identify because—compared to other churches—it is not declining noticeably, or its slowing growth rate doesn't raise any flags.

To the uneducated eye the Accelerated Growth church appears successful. Consequently it's easy to overlook and fail to ask the questions or push for the improvements that will lead to another chapter of increased contribution to its community.

R=Realignment—As with the Accelerated Growth, this church requires a more discerning look. Though declining numerically, this church displays a strong balance sheet; never failing to pay its bills, it may possess significant financial reserves. However, the healthy financial condition masks the precipitous decline in numbers and ageing membership. The leadership is basically satisfied with the church's ministry and future, focused on the bottom line of, "we're paying our bills." With regard to the numerical decline there's a misguided assumption that "things will change" or "things will get better in time." Often, the leadership gravitates toward specific silos of concern with little unity around a common strategy or compelling mission. A requirement for success is for the church to realign its ministries and budgeting priorities with a clearly defined vision for the future.

S=Successful, Strong—This kind of church is much easier, because it produces good ministry and metrics and the spiritual fruit found throughout the ecclesiology of the New Testament. It's well known within its tribe as well as its community. High-caliber leadership displays maturity, focusing on common goals, strategies, and mission.

It's worth noting, as Watkins does, that almost any organization going through a transition has some hybrid combination of the STARS profile, especially older churches that may have strong mixtures of Turnaround and Realignment. Remember, the purpose of the profile is not to put the church in a box but rather to have a common language to *communicate the strategy* to move the church forward during and following the transition.

> COACHING TIP: Supervisors and selection or personnel committees must take into account the unique challenges faced by the incoming pastor and the receiving congregation and manage the transition accordingly . . . best done with consultation and professional coaching.

Is there any doubt that the first few steps in the Changeover Zone matter a great deal? And the early steps always include learning in depth about the church's DNA and how to talk about it with common language to all parties involved in the transition.

The STARS profile provides a way to understand the setting and DNA of a church going through a transition. To increase understanding and common language, two additional tools have proved beneficial. These tools are in the form of questions.

The first question has to do with the life cycle in which each church finds itself: Where is the church in its life cycle? Birth? Growth? Maturity? Aging? Decline? Near death? Again, the issue here isn't to judge, but to get all parties working toward consensus so that conversation will truly inform decisions about the pastoral leadership, strategies, and tactics employed.

The second question has to do with the "emotional state" of each church: Due to the current pastor departing, where is the church in its grieving process? When a church says "goodbye" to its pastor, most often the congregation experiences a sense of loss and experiences the emotion of grief. These stages of grief are commonly known as denial, anger, depression, negotiation, and acceptance. Even if a church is glad about the pastor leaving (saying "good riddance" more than "goodbye"), it will still go through the various stages of grief. As it should be, this is a moving target—always changing and never static.

The five stages of grief are not new, but incoming pastors often ignore this dynamic. The supervisor cannot let the incoming pastor do so. This topic must be front and center. The supervisor will want to encourage the incoming pastor to ask two questions: (1) What is the emotional state of the congregation? (2) What stage are they in?

It is beneficial for the supervisor and the respective pastors and the church to have a common way to characterize the church as it enters the Changeover Zone. Is it in Denial? Anger? Depression? Negotiation? Acceptance? As with grieving humans, the church as a corporate body will go through the various stages in different ways and at different times. Similarly, individuals—depending upon their relationship with the departing pastor—are processing through these stages. The incoming pastor will want to remain alert to these nuances and respond appropriately.

To summarize, great transitions are more likely when the supervisor(s), church leadership, and departing and incoming pastors have had ample conversation toward agreement on and understanding of: (a) identifying the respective church within the STARS profile (or a similar profile) and (b) a common-language discussion about where the church is in its life cycle, and where it is related to the stages of grief. Then the supervisors, pastors, and church can turn to those strategies and tactics most likely to be effective and implemented by the church. In this preparation phase, the supervisor might employ clarifying questions that may lead to the right use of *tactics*, making for a smooth transition. Questions such as, What is . . .

causing the transition?

the context of the transition?

the emotional state of the church?

the consideration(s) of the mission field?

the caliber of potential successors?

Positioning

For a relay race, the coach assumes the positioned runners know their respective roles, have trained appropriately, and are highly motivated to succeed.

Hopefully, every supervisor can carry similar assumptions when seeking to position a pastor. However, as any track coach knows, some runners handle curves better; others excel in straightaways; others burst out of the starting block better; others seem to close to the finish line better. Simply put, the coach must position each runner and stay informed by understanding and assessing how best to match the runners' strengths, skills, and abilities to the particular need in the race. Positioning is a matter of matching each runner to the situation. The word "positioning" is a more neutral term and thus more appropriate than a word like "assessing." For supervisors in pastoral transitions, "positioning" is not judging the merits of a pastor's abilities or call to ministry; it is matching the right pastor with the right situation at the right time.

Promoting

Regardless of the reasons for the transition or the age of the church, there will be anxiety about the change of leadership in a local church. The more successful a church has been in bringing in new people, the more important this function will be. Why? Because when a church is successfully reaching the mission field and bringing in new people, it will be more and more populated by those "outside of, or new to, the tribe," and thus may be unfamiliar with the protocol involved in a pastoral change. That is to say, the more a church grows numerically the less its constituents will have a history with or understanding of the way pastoral changes occur. The corporate history inherent in denominational churches founded in the 1950s through the turn of the century can no longer be counted on to verify, "This is the way we change pastors here." The supervisor has to promote this change with enthusiasm, confidence, and integrity. Even if the change is happening in, or because of, bad circumstances, the supervisor must promote the change as a way to bring about health, new beginnings, and a positive turning point for the church. (Later chapters will contain some techniques to promote the change that will greatly reduce the anxiety level.)

Preventing

Often, the exhilaration of a pastoral transition, the "handoff," blinds all concerned to ironing out the details. And as is commonly known, the devil is in the details. Behind the focal point of the "exchange," every supervisor faces the myriad details that must be cared for to prevent confusion, frustration, and anger when a transition takes place. There must be absolute clarity and communication between all parties regarding such things as:

- Compensation specifics

- Pension, insurance, and other benefits

- Start dates

- Current personnel and expectations

- Budget details of the church

- Context of the transition

- Why the new pastor is a good match

- New pastor's strengths and areas of growth (DISC, Birkman, or other assessment results)

- Pastor's previously scheduled commitments that might affect first few months or year

- Pastor's family expectations regarding participation in the church

Clarity and communication on all the above prevent some of the missteps that get in the way of the incoming pastor getting off to a running start and that may result in a botched handoff. Taking care of the logistic details must be done, much like a punch list used for planning. This prevents significant misunderstandings when hammered out ahead of time.

In certain cases, due to time limitations or other issues, addressing the logistical concerns is the only step taken by all parties, including supervisors. Doing so leaves everyone with an empty feeling and guarantees a botched handoff.

Propelling

It is not enough simply to plan for and work toward a smooth transition. In the relay race each runner is expected to stay in training and to perform conditioning exercises; they follow nutritional diets and learn the value of healthy resources to keep in shape for their race. What propels them forward in the race is the quality of support and resources *available between races.*

In the pastoral transition, what propels the incoming pastor for success—especially in the Changeover Zone—is the quality of continuous and compelling resources provided to the pastor for success (see the appendix for reading and training materials). Imagine, for instance, if an approved facilitator/trainer could lead a structured discussion with those pastors moving, regarding resources dealing with pastoral transition. Increasingly, such forums are available and help "propel" the transition forward and create goodwill and trust between the pastor, church, and supervisors. Ideally, such transition discussions would not be initiated *only* at the time of transition but as ongoing continuing education for pastors and churches throughout the year. Sadly, many pastors and churches go through critical transitions with very limited, if any, training, support, and resources.

A successful transition takes work and effort in the Changeover Zone and beyond! Given the frequency of pastoral transitions, it is work well worth the time and focus of supervisors.

Chapter 4

The Role of Church Leaders

Saying "Goodbye" and Saying "Hello"

The five S's of sports training are: Stamina, Speed, Strength, Skill, and
Spirit but the greatest of these is Spirit.

—Ken Doherty

Pastoral transitions come in all sizes and under all circumstances: some good and some with intense pain, angst, and even embarrassment. Whatever the circumstance, church leaders must keep the spirit of the church positive and forward looking so that the church can "stay the course" during a time of anxiety and uncertainty. If the church drifts toward despair, anger, fear, or worry over what will happen, or becomes obsessed with disappointment at losing their dearly loved pastor—spirits will sag and the church will veer off course.

So as the church says, "goodbye" to its departing pastor and "hello" to the new incoming pastor, the leadership must adopt a laser-like focus on the transition, new hope, new opportunities, new life, and new energy that will drive the church into a compelling future chapter of its ministry.

During a pastoral transition private meetings abound. Due to the sensitive nature of the topic and confidentiality issues, most meetings remain out of the public eye. Persons are discussed, introductions made, and difficult topics negotiated. However, once the details have been finalized and decisions made, the transition must now make its way into the public arena. This transition to the public arena assumes that announcements have gone out to the church about the transition.

It's during the "going public" phase of the Changeover Zone that church leadership must manage in a way that makes for a smooth and seamless handoff during a pastoral change. In most contexts, this critical element that helps maintain the spirit of the church happens during the worship service as the church says "Goodbye" and "Hello" at the same time.

Unfortunately, due to the lack of experience with pastoral transitions, many churches overlook how to say "goodbye" and "hello," missing out on the opportunities that will propel the church out of the Changeover Zone and into a new future of dynamic growth. So here are a few tips.

Rally the Troops

The younger the church in a new church setting (or the longer the length of time since the last transition in a long-tenured pastorate), the more shock experienced in the congregation. That shock will play itself out in different ways by different people at different times...much like the stages of grief after the loss of a loved one.

Therefore, the primary function of church leadership is to rally the troops. This is done by first maintaining a calm presence, reminding and reassuring the church that God is in control. While there are numerous business resources on leadership that both model and suggest transition approaches that can benefit a church, ultimately the transition process for a church in the Changeover Zone requires prayerful dependence on God who holds the promise of the future.

Second, rally *around* Bible study and *in* prayer. This transition time affords the church leaders to call for a church-wide movement of prayer, a rally of prayer vigils, prayer groups, prayer chains, online devotionals, and prayer opportunities. The leaders ask the entire congregation to look up and call on the Lord for clarity, direction, and confidence as it enters the Changeover Zone.

Third, it's critically important to rally the church by communicating clearly, effectively, positively, and enthusiastically about the transition. To the degree that the church leadership is willing and able to convey confidence in the "system" and in the new pastor, and in the church's ability to handle the transition, the more likely it will experience a smooth transition.

Recruit

The church leaders also see this as a significant opportunity to recruit new people—especially younger people—into some specific, short-term area of ministry. And, with effective mentoring, many of these new recruits can be guided into more extensive service in the days and years ahead. Practice these three key principles in recruiting for the "goodbye" and "hello" events.

First, Make It Fun

Starting four or five weeks out, the church's personnel committee chair, the worship leader, and the departing pastor agree to set aside five minutes at the end of each service to talk about saying goodbye to the pastor. This can be made fun and memorable when the pastor is excused so the church family can talk in private. In the case of one pastor who was departing after eighteen years, each week a member of the personnel committee ceremoniously escorted the pastor out of the sanctuary for five minutes. People clapped and whistled as the pastor was led out each Sunday. Then, in the pastor's absence the designated Personnel spokesperson would facilitate the congregation in planning the pastor's "goodbye." At the end of the five minutes the pastor was escorted back in to conclude the worship service.

From the platform, the facilitator presented the five minutes in a manner that said:

"We're gonna have a lot of fun with this, and we want our pastor to be completely surprised. Can I get your agreement that we'll keep this just amongst ourselves? [This kind of fun and drama engages everyone in the church; but especially younger people seem to enjoy this.]

"We're gonna need some really good help with all this. None of us on the personnel committee are good at planning big events, but I'm guessing someone here today is. We need you to step up, even if you've never helped the church out with anything like this before. This is short-term; it will only last a few weeks, but it has to be somebody with great organizational skills and who likes surprises and likes to have lots of fun.

"Now, take a look at the card we're distributing. It has listed on it some ways you can help. We are going to need five teams of at least five people each. Let us know how you can help say 'goodbye' to our pastor and 'hello' to our new pastor. Someone on the personnel committee will work with each team, but we really are counting on the good folks who love this church to make all this happen. Before our pastor's final week, we'll be involving almost all of you here this morning somehow. And we're gonna have lots of fun!"

Notice how important it is to recruit. Everybody knows this is short-term; it isn't like the recruitment of a Sunday school teacher for the summer that ends up being a lifetime commitment. People—especially newer people to the church—can be assured this is truly short-term. But it may well yield long-term results of getting someone involved for the very first time.

The reason to recruit while in the Changeover Zone is not simply to expand the labor pool. One of the best ways to assimilate new people into a church is to offer specific short-term tasks, especially when it affords the opportunity to meet people in the church. It is in the doing that many people will make new friends and begin new relationships, which is critical to the purpose of a church and the gospel.

In many churches, it's also feasible that first-time guests will be in attendance. They don't know the departing pastor; they don't know the system of changing pastors; they don't know the incoming pastor; they don't even know the church yet... but what they can know is that they are sitting in a church thinking, *This sure is a thoughtful and fun church; I like this! I can relate to this; there's a lot of good stuff going on!*

Similarly, the "hello" events to welcome the incoming pastor and family frequently open the door to newer members or even guests in the church to become key players in welcoming the new leader.

Second, Make It Familiar

Most church members can empathize with both the departing and incoming pastors. Chances are they've experienced a vocational transition or two. They know what it's like to relocate a family to a different community for the sake of employment; they know what it's like to fit in to a new community and work situation. Even if they don't comprehend or appreciate the why or what of the pastoral change, they know that business leaders change jobs and positions and move on. Truth be known, most church members have more experience at transitions than most pastors.

The five-minute facilitator on the platform will want to make this transition something that the majority of the church can relate to, by allowing their empathy to open the door to helping out in the transition. Often the facilitator will say something like: "You all know what it's like to go through a big change, to move to a new city or to start a new job. Well, that's what our preacher is going through and that's what our new preacher and family are going through. So let's treat them like we would want to be treated in saying both goodbye and hello."

Third, Make It Unforgettable

Pastoral transitions can be miserable, if not planned out by the church leadership. To overcome this lethargy, the church leaders must work hard to make the transition a memorable time, one that people will not soon forget. In some cases, unforgettable transitions beget a church narrative that leads to a history of smooth and seamless handoffs in the Changeover Zone. See below some examples of ideas from churches, especially noting their creativity and intentionality:

- Memories: a collection photographs of every church the pastor has ever served, made into a beautiful quilt displaying each; photo albums assembled with care and class, including captions; a box full of thank-you notes and memory moments written by children, youth, and adults in the church; a community Bible signed by church members on the margins of the pages.

- Thanks: vacation or special trip package to a "bucket wish list" destination of pastor and family; money tree; gift certificates; a scrapbook of thanks and memories from community leaders and pastors of other churches in the community; an official proclamation by the governor, state assembly, and/or mayor of the city honoring the departing pastor.

- Needs: a gift of something the pastor and family may need— clergy robe or stole, dishes, furniture, electronics, and so forth.

- Family Members: don't forget the pastor's family: memory books with photos and messages from church members and children from the church for each of the children.

In addition, a pastoral change is a "marker moment" for a church. Many congregants will reference significant moments in their life to the arrival of a new pastor. It is not uncommon to hear comments such as: "We were the first family to join when Pastor Sheila arrived."

Reorient

A tougher but essential task of church leadership is to introduce the congregation to a new leader. When church members are so in love with the departing pastor that they cannot reorient around the incoming one, they will have a hard time moving positively into the future. This reorientation process challenges the church leaders, as they also are learning a new personality and a new leadership style. Often they will reach out to a specialist who serves to coach them through its various stages of grief over losing their pastor and their leader.

The church leadership must encourage the incoming pastor to ask questions and push the status quo, giving the new pastor permission to try some new things and defend the pastor to those in the congregation who simply want business as usual and make statements like: "We've always done it this way."

This does not mean the church must or should sacrifice its identity, vision, or mission for the sake of the incoming pastor's agenda. It does mean that the church and new pastor will be charging together out of the Changeover Zone and into the future.

Church leaders must pay attention to the remaining staff members—full and part time—who are in most cases grieving, some cases celebrating, but in all cases filled with anxiety about their future under the new pastor; in no case will they be indifferent to the leadership change.

The staff members may well feel slighted or overlooked; after all, they are people with real feelings. They work hard to make the ministry of the church happen and, in their own way, carry the baton during the transition. Church leaders must take care not to push them into the background. Find ways to recognize them publicly and privately as a group and each as an individual. Remember in all the celebrating of departures and arrivals, not everybody is leaving: essential team members are "holding down the fort."

How church leaders act in the Changeover Zone sets the stage for how the church responds to opportunities for identifying new leadership, reinvigorating itself, and charging into the future.

As one of eight children, it was always special for me to visit grandparents in rural Illinois. As our station wagon rumbled down the chalky county road to their house, we would watch Grandma come out the front door with a huge bright smile. She was a rotund woman upon greeting you would grab the bottom of her apron, lift it upward, and wave it excitedly toward the car, saying, "Hello! Hello! Hello!"

After our visit we would pile back into the car to leave, and there would be Grandma with that big smile, clutching her apron in the same way, only this time she shouted, "Goodbye!" Now, that might be because she was happy to see eight kids leaving; but whatever it was, I always marveled that she said hello and goodbye with the same loving enthusiasm.

This childhood memory captures the essence of the church in a transition: saying goodbye and saying hello with the same loving enthusiasm.

Chapter 5

The Role of the Departing Pastor

A Smooth and Seamless Handoff

Real athletes run; others just play games.
—T-shirt at a track meet

In track, relay runners are characterized as either the "incoming" or the "outgoing" and at different times in different races are expected to play either part. This same understanding is critical for pastoral transitions. At various times over a ministry career, a pastor will either be handing the baton off or receiving it. Good pastoral leadership requires competency in both roles. Imagine what it could look like for pastors to go through seminars and workshops on pastoral transitions in constructive ways. Imagine what it might look like if those involved in transition, both overseers and pastors, benefit from a culture that educates, trains, and coaches the process of transition in ways that reduce the angst and anxiety and promote a healthier giving and receiving of the baton.

Who carries the baton in the pastoral transition? The departing pastor! Charging full speed into the Changeover Zone, departing pastors must set aside ego and realize that if the handoff is executed poorly, it hurts the whole team: the pastors, the church, and the supervisors.

Departing pastors must see themselves as running into the Changeover Zone, 100 percent committed to success in passing the baton. When they see themselves as the "incoming" runner—coming into a specific time frame known as the Changeover Zone with specific responsibilities, *then* they will enthusiastically put in the time, work, and effort to make it a smooth and seamless handoff. When departing pastors see themselves as charging into the last leg of their tenure—not just "biding their time till it's time to go"—they will produce culture change, because they will enter the Changeover Zone and view it as a specific, definable role to facilitate passing the baton on to their successor.

Departing pastors who exhibit good exit strategy behaviors are obsessed with making a smooth transition in the Changeover Zone. They know that a dropped baton or sloppy handoff jeopardizes everything. In too many transitions the baton is dropped because the departing pastor downplays their role in helping the new pastor get off to a running start, or in how well the church responds to the transition. Successful departing pastors discard a "that's their problem" mentality and exchange it for one that asks "what can we do to make this great?"

The daunting reality for the pastors (both departing and arriving) involved in the Changeover Zone is that most of the time the pastors are working two roles simultaneously: saying goodbye and saying hello. The pastors are departing their current church and, unless retiring or otherwise leaving pastoral ministry, at the same time preparing for a new church—learning a new congregation, culture, and ministry setting. Time demands are stretched; attention and focus are split in this pressure-filled juggling act. Fortunately, this relay race is a sprint and not a marathon

How Departing Pastors Help Their Successor and the Church

"Maroon Colonies" are what archeologists call the unique settlements they are excavating in the Great Dismal Swamp National Park, bordering Virginia and North Carolina. The Underground Railroad snaked through its unknown dangers and unending miles of dense undergrowth, howling wildlife, biting insects, and fog thicker than the porridge most of the escaping slaves ate for their daily meal. It was a place of transition: get through it and the other side offered hope, freedom, and a future. Many slave traders were hesitant to venture in, fearing its foreboding vastness and reputation for being haunted.

But the protection it afforded—which made the transition from slavery to freedom possible—became something altogether different for thousands of escaping slaves over the years. That's why archeologists are now finding hundreds of rough villages built by slaves who entered the swamp but never came out. Instead of journeying on, they settled in.

Amazingly, even while living in constant fear of bloodhounds and slave traders and the daunting insects and wildlife, they still managed to establish settlements first meant to be temporary but later became permanent. The ruins of these maroon colonies are still being excavated today, revealing that generations dwelled in circumstances almost as dire as living in slavery.

"Maroon colonies" offer a way to talk about poor pastoral transitions and how they can negatively effect the church. Pastors and churches going through transitions often experience having to journey through a great dismal swamp in which people hang around in hopelessness, wondering if they'll ever come out on the other side. They didn't plan on it, but inadvertently they became tethered to the past and are unable to transition to a new future under a new pastor. They remain hidden in maroon colonies, stuck in some particular time in the church's history—remembering the "good old days"—devoted to some former pastor and previous era. Some folks remain hidden in Sunday school classes and special groups still devoted to the past, sometimes holding on to tenures of former pastors many years past.

Pastors often report that "great dismal swamp" feeling—that their new church is filled with fog and lurking unknown dangers that can erupt at any decision they make, any initiative they take, any statement they utter, or any sermon they deliver. Instead of people journeying on, they settle in the past. And such a swampy culture can make everyone's life miserable.

The good news is that no church needs to make a maroon colony in the great dismal swamp. And one of the best guides to help the church not settle into the great dismal swamp of the past is the departing pastor. Departing pastors enter into the Changeover Zone carrying a checklist of five specific behaviors that increase chances for success and help the church navigate through the transition on its way to a new future:

Engage—Be sincere, genuine, and intentional while engaging the congregation in both a personal and professional way. Personalize the transition and make it real—own the situation, but never blame the transition on the "system" or other external forces. Departing pastors have a chance to model faith and integrity by receiving and accepting the move with faith and integrity, acknowledging and affirming God's hand in it. If they have initiated the transition, the departing pastor can create a "faith narrative" to help the congregation absorb the reasons for her or his departure. Unfortunately, some departing pastors can be rather duplicitous about how the change came about and this serves no purpose. People in pews are used to job changes; draw on that common experience in a positive way with statements such as, "What I'll be doing next…"; "What I learned here that I'll take with me…"; "What you folks taught me…"

Professionalize—Make this as professional a transition as anyone in the congregation would want to see in their professional career life. Like the runner charging into the changeover zone, the departing pastor charges into the concluding days with intentionality and gusto: loose ends are tied up; records and statistical data are in order; and ministry projects are attended to with a minimal amount of things dropping through the cracks. Departing pastors often make it a part of their daily agenda to do something that will make life easier for the successor. All this serves to lay a firm foundation for the pastor.

Enrich—This is a great teaching moment about how pastoral changes are done within the church's context. Some systems are more complex and interconnected; other systems may be simpler and more local-church oriented. But whatever it is, this is not a time to apologize or blame. Instead, the departing pastor embraces it and casts vision for the church's future under new leadership: passing the baton. This enrichment function must be done publicly in closing sermons, Bible studies, and meetings as well as in personal, private conversations and other settings.

Endear—The departing pastor helps endear the congregation to the new pastor better than anyone else. Coach Tony Miller of the Southern Methodist University sprint team emphasizes that the two most critical elements to having success in the changeover zone are trust and positioning. "The outgoing runner has to have absolute trust that the incoming runner will be at the right speed, and perform the hand-off at the right time in the right way," says Coach Miller, adding, "without trust, the team falters, losing precious momentum...and ultimately the race." Tony is not only the track coach but also an active church leader. So he shared this bit of wisdom:

> In my church, the outgoing pastor "grooms" the successor, so they have developed great trust. But in some churches, the new pastor is "assigned" or "appointed" or comes from far away. So the same degree of "grooming" isn't able to happen. But if you can't really groom your successor, at least groom the "relationship" with your successor! Be intentional. Do what our sprint team kids do when new athletes come in for the academic year: spend time outside the track with each other; quickly get to know the other runners—their strengths, and interests, and passion. *You don't have trust without grooming relationships.* So I'd recommend in churches where you can't directly groom your successor, at least spend intentional time grooming a relationship before you try to hand off the baton!

"Grooming" doesn't simply mean transferring information and techniques from one pastor to the next. Grooming is discipling. It is pouring one's heart and soul into another person, just as Jesus did. In those groups that do not practice planned successions, this is harder to do; but it is still the responsibility of departing pastors to do their best to groom a relationship with the successor whenever, however, and wherever possible. This doesn't need to take a long time (though the longer the better), but it does require attention and intentionality. This relationship building accelerates the "endearing" of the incoming pastor within the congregation and happens in a number of ways that can successfully be done by the departing pastor.

First, departing pastors develop a plan that introduces their successor in as many ways as possible. By far, the best way—technology allowing—is via video. Both the departing pastor and the incoming pastor appear together in several introductory videos to be shown during worship and at church meetings and gatherings. The most effective ones, though simply made, are creative, funny, interesting, and compelling. To see samples, visit www.Oziercoaching.org. In addition to video, many churches use simple techniques like "Five Fun Facts" or "Two Truths and a Lie" included in morning worship for three or four Sundays leading up to the new pastor's arrival. The departing pastor adopts the role of game-show host for this brief, fun, interactive time.

Encourage—Departing pastors realize their church faces a great deal of stress and anxiety when going into the Changeover Zone and thus work overtime to encourage people to love their new pastor. The departing pastor encourages the church to meet the challenges of the future, continue vital ministries, and start new ones. Remind, remind, and remind that this is kingdom business!

End—Departing pastors close the pastor/parishioner relationships and friendships with planning and sensitivity, ever mindful that proper goodbyes permit their successor to form similar bonds. Recall what Coach Tony has learned as a track coach: it takes trust and positioning. It is the responsibility of the supervisor to position pastors in the best places to be successful; it is the responsibility of the departing pastor to build the trust relationship with the incoming pastor, helping position the successor for success by gracefully and intentionally "ending" pastoral relationships with close members of the congregation. Robert Kaylor in *Your Best Move* speaks about the importance of conducting an "exit interview"[1] and includes helpful questions and tips for leaving in the appendix section.[2]

Note: In rare but painful circumstances, the departing pastor may simply not be a gracious or thoughtful person; perhaps the departing pastor, for a variety of reasons, may already be gone from the church before the incoming pastor arrives. Sadly, there are times when the departing pastor has been removed because of improper behavior. In these cases, the supervisor must step up and either perform the functions of the departing pastor or see to it that an intentional interim pastor is in place to fulfill all of these functions.

Chapter 6

The Role of the Incoming Pastor

Taking the Baton

You have a choice. You can throw in the towel, or you can use it to wipe the sweat off your face.

—Gatorade advertisement

W illiam felt confident about going to his new church. He had weathered his two previous assignments quite well and Christ Church seemed about the same—maybe a little larger, bespeaking the promotion he felt was coming his way. His supervisor assured him that the church offered ample opportunity for his gifts to flourish and the church to move forward. In his early interviews, the personnel committee seemed eager to have him and the "church profile" statement appealed to him: "We want to grow and continue in discipleship." Everyone seemed eager for a new chapter. After all, isn't that what each church and minister want—a successful new chapter? Yes, as he entered into the Changeover Zone, William felt good.

As often happens, William did little to prepare himself while waiting to receive the baton in the Changeover Zone other than a cursory look at the church and community. His practice, for which he prided himself, was to reserve judgment, keep an open mind, treat everyone the same, give everyone a chance, and most certainly not inquire of others ahead of time for fear of appearing "too eager." His approach had worked in previous churches, and he had no reason to assume it wouldn't in this one also.

But not this time. From the moment he received the baton, he found himself weighed down. And with each passing month, the distance between him and the church leaders widened, so much so that he began to feel not just left behind but that he was running in a different race. The baton became increasingly hard to carry, and in several key turns, somebody had dropped it. What had gone so terribly wrong? Though not new to ministry, William made the classical transition mistake: he evaluated his new church based on previous church experiences; he looked at the future through his lens of the past. Like others before him, William missed the memo, "Not all churches are the same."

In previous Changeover Zones, his instincts and habits had served him well. This time all systems failed miserably. After three years, William departed, a broken and exhausted pastor. We have discovered that as the baton is received in the Changeover Zone, the incoming minister must have a better understanding of what's in it: namely, the DNA of the welcoming church. And, as was the case with William, sometimes the passing of the baton proves much more difficult than assumed, expected, or hoped for. Unfortunately, when ill-prepared hands attempt the handoff exchange, serious consequences can come in rapid, often debilitating sequence, which diminishes the chances of the new pastor to perform equal to previous experiences.

As they stand in the Changeover Zone awaiting the baton, how can incoming pastors prepare themselves to receive the handoff? They cannot afford to rely solely on their own instincts or the observations of others. They must do their homework. One way to prepare is to make a wholehearted commitment to learning and analyzing the DNA of the welcoming church. When we train pastors for the Changeover Zone, we encourage them to ask, "What's in the baton?" Of course, the pastor cannot know everything in it, but there are a few things the pastor can do, so that when they receive it officially, they have a heads-up and a general course of action to follow.

In chapter 2, we shared the STARS profile to be used by supervisors. The incoming pastor must listen carefully to the supervisor's thoughts on this but perform their own analysis. After all, it is rare that supervisors will actually know as much about a church as they should know, and there are even times when supervisors may not paint a correct picture of the church for the incoming pastor.

While no one person or group (or church) enjoys being put in a box, the following analysis will prove quite helpful, at least to get a realistic view of the situation and understanding of the church's DNA. Each type of church requires different—but doable—leadership styles and tactical approaches. The key to a smooth transition is: (1) having a clear and agreed-upon understanding of the church's context and culture, (2) matching the right leadership style to the church's needs, and (3) being able to communicate with common language to all parties involved.

We call this the "Five Kinds of Churches": Heritage, Toxic, Vital, Accident, and Founder's. Here is a brief description of each:

(1) **The Heritage Church** has enjoyed a long history of many decades producing healthy fruit: baptisms/new professions of faith; spiritual formation/education; culture of generosity/stewardship; vibrant missions; and witness and voice in the public arena. Many in the community have experienced these fruits firsthand, and others still trace the beginning of their spiritual journey to the heritage church.

However, over time the community context and demographics surrounding the heritage church begins to change, and quite understandably, the church trends toward being isolated from its changing community. A myriad of reasons may apply, but most often this happens through the normal migration that follows its citizens: some die, some move away, some change their church habits, and others move in. Consequently, the number of members diminishes and what was once a flourishing church now finds itself grieving the loss that accompanies numerical decline. While the membership rolls may say "x" amount, the actual attendance says something quite different.

Without some intentional intervention process—usually involving consulting and coaching with skilled "outside eyes"—the heritage church becomes a shell of its former self. Denial runs deep and as decades pass, desperation accumulates, and with it, a heightened expectation. And each time there is a change of pastoral leadership, the baton grows heavier.

The reality is that in increasingly more situations, the heritage church may be on the verge of becoming a "legacy church," defined as: when the members recognize they can no longer provide viable ministry and so choose to (a) close and allow their facility to be "repositioned" and restarted as a new church to meet the changing demographics, or (b) close and allow their assets to be directed to start a new church to reach new people in some other location.

While this sacrificial act is a good and missional decision, not every heritage church is destined to become a legacy church. Heritage churches can in fact "turn around" under the right strategy, tactics, and leadership. Jim Griffith's popular weekend workshop "Reach New People" is specifically designed to bring about new energy in heritage churches.

(2) **The Toxic Church** also possesses a long history of fruit. However this fruit differs quite differently from the heritage church. Consultants summarize this fruit in one word: abuse. The toxic church abuses the minister, the minister's family, each other, the community—virtually anything and anyone it encounters. And in all too frequent cases, it has for many

decades displayed a remarkable ability to survive the effects of such destructive behavior.

Occasionally, to everyone's surprise, every once in a great while (once a decade?), for a brief period (three to six months) the spirit of God breaks through and begins to work on the hearts of a few. Toxic churches view such occurrences as "interruptions," so as quickly as the Spirit surfaces, its effects are as quickly extinguished. Normalcy—and not in a good or healthy way—returns.

The unsuspecting minister who lacks a theology of evil will not survive long in such a setting. Sadly, all too often being placed in these settings can dash the pastor's morale to greatly diminish her or his future ministry and sometimes even drive the pastor out of the ministry.

(3) **The Vital Church** follows the Supreme Court Justice's quip, "You'll know it when you see it!" Its history mirrors that of the heritage church, but with one exception: when the vital church begins to encounter isolation, the leaders call a halt to business as usual and ask, "What's happening and what do we need to change?"

This intervention disrupts the normalcy of "we've always done it that way" and leads the church through the force field of resistance to new possibilities. After making this move, the vital church continues on its way, reaching ever more people and expanding its influence for Christ to the next generation of disciples.

(4) **The Accident Church** may be characterized as a generally good, healthy church that has suffered an "accident." At times, in a church's history, uninvited actions or unintended circumstances create such disruption in a church that it becomes damaged, sometimes traumatized for generations. Many things can cause this: from pastoral "indiscretions" to something as innocent as a notice from the Federal Highway Department informing the church of a road change that will come through the church's fellowship hall. For whatever reason, vitality and good health are interrupted and damage occurs with lasting results. No one wanted it, no one invited it, and no one predicted or expected it. It just happened.

(5) **The Founder's Church** occupies a category altogether different. This church has had only one pastor, its founder. Similar dynamics also apply to a church that has had a "long-tenured" pastor—one who has occupied the pulpit for ten, twenty, thirty, or forty years. That is to say, founder's churches have had either the original founder, or a pastor who has occupied the pulpit so long that few can remember the previous pastor, and almost everyone identifies the pastor as the keystone of their spiritual journey.

Not surprisingly, the church members have a special connection to this pastor. To some, their pastor is the only pastor they've ever known. This pastor sat with them through a family trauma, initiated them into the faith, walked with them deeply into the path of discipleship. In virtually every circumstance of a founder, the outgoing pastor's role in the lives of the congregation is viewed and remembered as "larger than life."

Regardless of what kind of church you are moving to, you can do far more than you think as the new pastor of a church. This is your opportunity to learn from your past experiences—good and bad; this may even be a time to "reinvent" yourself and your ministry to meet new challenges and circumstances. God called you into the ministry for specific reasons, and this new setting may allow your unique gifts and graces an opportunity to burst out in exciting, faithful ways.

COACHING TIP: For those pastors moving to an accident church, the incoming minister must know that people are not "challenged" or inspired through an accident. They are cared for.

Frequently, pastors going to a new church, especially if it is viewed as a "good move," report that jealous colleagues voice skepticism and doubts that you should be the one to go to this particular church. You'll probably have some self-doubts along the way as well. This is your chance to show doubters that you have what it takes to be an effective pastor in this new situation . . . even if the doubter is yourself!

Being mocked for her age and chastised in the press because she was a "mother who should be staying home with her child" didn't stop Fanny Blankers-Koen from stunning the world in the 1948 London Olympics. She earned four gold medals, including the 4 x 100 and 4 x 400 relays and popularly became known as "the flying housewife."

That she was one of the fastest women who ever lived didn't make her journey any easier: "I got very many bad letters, people writing that I must stay home with my children and that I should not be allowed to run on a track with—how do you say it?—short trousers," she said in the *New York Times* in 1982. "One newspaperman wrote that I was too old to run, that I should stay at home and take care of my children. When I got to London, I pointed my finger at him and I said, 'I show you.'"[1]

She did show him and the world, but before she could break world records and break through cultural and social barriers, she first had to overcome her own self-doubts and make the decision to enter the 1948 Olympics as a thirty-year-old mother. Her feisty spirit and fiery determination shattered cultural conceptions about age and feminism that had defined the world. "The Flying Housewife" became a pioneer and icon for culture change that changed the world. Her impact was far greater than she could have ever dreamt!

For incoming pastors to have a lasting impact that exceeds expectations, it helps to get started right: grabbing the baton and charging out of the Changeover Zone with confidence and determination, overcoming fears, obstacles, and barriers.

Earlier we explained how the supervisor or personnel committee can effectively use the STARS profile, the "Life Cycle," and the "Stages of Grief" to set the strategy for a good pastoral transition. It is important to note that the incoming pastor must similarly apply these same tools to nearly every *aspect and system* of their new church. (For instance, the STARS profile: Startup, Turnaround, Accelerated Growth, Realignment, Successful, Strong). Using this common language helps facilitate productive conversations with supervisors and church leaders. As we mentioned earlier, employing this profile will help the incoming pastor determine *strategy*, before jumping into *tactics*. An incoming pastor may well discover that the hospitality ministry needs a *turnaround*, while a needed "quick win" new ministry like providing a household repair ministry to the elderly would be a *start-up*. Stewardship may have been gradually increasing every year, but the pastor senses it could and should be an area of *accelerated growth*. The staff and leadership may be in need of some *realignment*, while the small group ministry may be *successful, strong*.

The incoming pastor will be well served to understand which areas of the church would fall into each of the STARS profile, then analyze where it is in the "Five Kinds of Churches," and then act accordingly. Once the strategic thinking has begun, the incoming pastor can begin to address specific tactics, entering the Changeover Zone carrying a checklist of six specific behaviors that increase the odds of a smooth and successful transition.

Acquaint: The incoming pastor must get acquainted with the church, the community, and the people by every means possible, especially through studying church and community websites as well as "mission-field exegesis." That is, incoming pastors must immerse themselves in the mission field by

- getting acquainted with key leaders and influencers (fire and police chiefs, school principals, pastors, local business owners, etc.)

- making intentional visits to places of note in the community (charitable organizations, schools, helping agencies, gathering spots for the public, etc.)

- participating in civic, social, school, and public events happening in the community (arts, community initiatives, sports, etc.)

Accentuate: The incoming pastor must accentuate the positive. Some "no-no's" include *never* criticizing or second-guessing the predecessor or speak poorly of the church or previous pastors. Incoming pastors sometime have to work to stay positive and find ways to show appreciation by becoming champions of "thanking" and expressing gratitude in every public setting, including and especially from the Sunday morning platform. While done spontaneously, most often these expressions are well thought out, expressing gratitude and effusive thanks to a particular person or group serving in the church. This is done each and every Sunday in worship and at every opportunity in meetings or other events that occur during the week. One of the key roles of a new pastor is to "start the applause" when it comes to thanking others. Gushing praise and showing thanks will cover a multitude of mistakes during the transition.

Analyze: The incoming pastor dons the "analyst" hat to analyze the church, its context, the community's needs, and—as mentioned at the start of this chapter—the impact of the church to date. In the words of Jim Collins, this means being "rigorous not ruthless."[2] Analyzing is not to be confused with "judging." Be objective, clear, nonjudgmental, and humble in analyzing the context. Wisely involve and include others in the analytical behavior. The smartest and safest way is to quickly lead the church into some kind of well-structured process of "learning together." (For example, a congregational transformation process like "The Healthy Church Initiative" or church leadership workshops like "How to Reach New People." Less intensive but quite productive would be a guided group study of such books as Patrick Lencioni's *The Advantage*.)

Anticipate: The incoming pastor must anticipate the anxieties, concerns, fears, and worries of the church and individuals within the church as they receive their new pastor. Empathy allows the incoming pastor to identify with the congregation. There will be grief, and in some cases, jubilation. The emotional state of the congregation is never far from the incoming pastor's radar. It is oftentimes helpful to mention in morning worship the stages of grief (denial, anger, negotiating, depression, and acceptance) and acknowledge that people go through the stages at different times and in different ways. It is even more important for you as the new pastor to realize that, as they go through the stages of grief, some people will "act out"—just as a child might do at the loss of a parent or sibling. The new pastor must guard against internalizing such behaviors or "taking them personally," as doing so will interfere with the ability to guide congregants through the stages.

Ask: The incoming pastor asks questions, lots of them, to better understand the culture of the church. This is critical. At this point, "asking the right questions" is more important than "giving the right answers." The monotonous practice of "ask, ask, ask" demonstrates the curiosity and depth of care the incoming pastor has for the church. Repetition of asking convinces the congregation their new pastor really does want to know them and their context: what their church is about, what the community needs, and what the leadership expectations may be. Inquiry is usually the new pastor's best friend.

Similar to asking are two additional twin A's: alert and aware. Incoming pastors must always have their radar up and be alert to nuanced situations developing, or to people's behaviors and subtle agendas. This is exhausting work. It means reading body language and other indicators of feelings below the surface on the part of congregants, guests, staff, leaders, supervisors, and community influencers.

At the same time, new pastors can become so consumed with "being alert" that they neglect "being aware," especially, being *self-aware*: When it comes to "asking," it is critical to set aside daily self-reflection time in which to reflect and ask:

- How am I coming across?

- Am I being genuine and authentic?

- Am I being sensitive, gracious, and courteous?

- Am I being too assertive, aggressive, or holier than thou?

- Are my behaviors what I hope to see in others?

During the transition, one of the most often voiced complaints about the incoming pastor is, "Our new pastor just doesn't seem very self-aware."

Answer: The incoming pastor seeks to answer the many questions that will come their way in a humble, but transparent, way. They avoid answering from a position of authority or superiority—the incoming pastor has to earn authority, and that takes time. Successful incoming pastors take a self-revelatory position that indicates: "It's not my agenda but the church's and God's and the mission field's, and I want to do everything possible to learn more about it."

In the changeover zone the runner receiving has a lane of twenty meters in which to receive the baton; for most runners this allows for about seven steps before they sprint out on their leg of the relay. Similarly in a pastoral transition, there are seven critical steps the new pastor must take to get off to a good running start:

1. Say goodbye to the previous church in a healthy way.

2. Get spiritually centered and prepare the family for change.

3. Manage all the pre-arrival protocols and logistics in a thorough way.

4. Learn mission field culture via church and community websites and demographics.

5. Say hello via (a) relational presence, (b) listening tour, (c) mission field immersion.

6. Develop strategy for the first one hundred days, built around relational intentionality.

7. Prepare a preaching plan for the first three months.

Some of these steps (1-4) take place *after* the new pastor is announced, but *before* his or her official ministry begins, usually the one hundred days prior to the announcement. Other steps (5-7) happen during the first one hundred days *after* the new pastor arrives. But these seven steps are what allow the new pastor to dig in, to gain traction, and to charge out.

Taking Care of Their Pastor; Taking Care of Yourself

Beginning to exit the Changeover Zone, the new pastor faces many demands and responsibilities, many of which are insurmountable and unattainable during the first one hundred days. How incoming pastors manage their family, their church, and themselves determines their ability to sustain the kind of effort needed in the early days. Successful incoming pastors set boundaries immediately by setting aside regular time for (a) family/personal time; (b) spiritual disciplines; and (c) regular exercise and workouts. They do not make themselves available to the congregation 24/7. It is perfectly okay to say—or have the pastor's administrative assistant say—"The pastor is not available at this time."

Incoming pastors practice healthy stewardship of time and boundaries at the outset of their arrival. They do not wait for it to "show up" some time in the future, after they have exhausted themselves in countless meetings to the detriment of everyone around them. This enhances the true credibility the new pastor gains to lead the flock in daily living.

Elizabeth Grace Saunders observes,

> The higher you go in your organization, the more the basics matter. You don't need less sleep, you need more—and to be far stricter about making it a priority. Being sleep deprived dramatically decreases your emotional control, decision-making ability, and productivity. You can't afford to have those compromised at the next level. You don't need less exercise, you need more—or to simply maintain a solid schedule of physical care if you're already staying in shape. Regular movement improves your health, your mood, and your energy levels. You don't need less time with your family, friends, and simply relaxing—you need more. This will give you the resilience to weather the stresses of ups and downs in your business, and the perspective that there is more to life than work.[3]

And this includes the business of ministry. For effective ways to maintain time management, see *Time Management for the Christian Leader* by Ken Willard.

Chapter   7

Creating a Culture of Accountability

You don't want to let anyone down.

—Manteo Mitchell

In the summer of 2012, along with other members of Team USA, Manteo Mitchell marched into The Stadium at Queen Elizabeth Olympic Park in London to celebrate the opening of the XXX Olympiad. A 400-meter sprinter, he had qualified to run the opening leg of the men's 4 x 400 meter relay. He was a long way from his hometown of Shelby, North Carolina.

Manteo quickly became a front running story of the Games. While running for Team USA in the prelims of the 4 x 400 meter relay, he heard a crack and felt pain. "It felt like somebody literally just snapped my leg in half. I felt it break." It was later revealed that Manteo did break his left fibula. No one would have begrudged him retiring from the race; after all he had just broken his leg! However, retiring from the race meant the U.S. would have no chance to qualify for the finals. Instead he marshaled from within all the determination from years of training and life and ran the last 200 meters, handing off the baton to his teammate.

His Team USA teammates continued on, running the last three legs. Bahamas won the heat, but the Americans qualified a close second, credited with exactly the same time as Bahamas, the fastest time in 2012.

Ironically, during the same heat, the Dominican Republic failed to make the baton exchange in the changeover zone.[1] Then halfway through the third leg, Jamaica's Jermaine Gonzales pulled a muscle and was unable to continue. Both teams disqualified.

41

Even though he was not able to compete in the final, Manteo stills wears his silver medal proudly, because had he quit the race, he and his teammates would have gone home empty-handed. After the ceremony back at the Olympic Village, Manteo said, "You don't want to let anyone down." Winning a relay race isn't easy. Along with skill and preparation it requires determination, commitment, and perseverance. And no small measure of accountability to one's teammates.

The same can be said of a pastoral transition when the baton is passed in the Changeover Zone. The incoming pastor receives the baton and charges into a new chapter of ministry, not wanting to let anyone down. Not the personnel committee that made the selection, not the departing pastor, and certainly not the expectant congregation.

If the new chapter unfolds badly, plenty of excuses can be made. However, if all parties possess a willingness to create a culture of accountability then a good handoff will result, which will lead to a successful transition. Nobody said it would be easy, but it is worth it.

In *Change the Culture, Change the Game*, Roger Connors and Tom Smith point out that one of the major occasions in the life of any organization that leads to significant cultural change and different results is the arrival of a new leader. The arrival of the incoming pastor is a leadership change that will always lead to some significant culture change in the church.

What would happen if pastors, churches, and judicatories developed a similar culture? Entering the Changeover Zone is an ideal time for all parties—church, new pastor, supervisor—to implement or strengthen a necessary culture of accountability. Once in place during the transition, this culture of accountability can spread and morph and become the DNA of the church's culture as well. Such churches, if members of a larger group, will broaden their impact to the leaders and supervisors who oversee it.

Unfortunately, too often the culture is finger-pointing and blaming for problems that invariably arise. This can be demotivating to the pastor, demoralizing to the church, and devastating to the credibility of supervisors. To enjoy a smoother handoff, look candidly at the culture of accountability by first reflecting on the systemic (or as some will say, bureaucratic) accountability, but don't overlook *personal accountability* on the part of each team player. A clear and consistent culture of accountability enables the organization to leverage "change" into increased effectiveness in ministry and relevance to the mission field.

Track coaches tell us that successful teams are characterized by their preparation, expectation, anticipation, communication, and execution. The first four of the following list give an indication of *systemic* accountability: Are the right people doing the right things in the right way?

Preparation—Everyone involved knows their respective role and how to do it with passion and excellence; they know how their role connects to the whole process and they take ownership for doing all they can for success.

Anticipation—Learn to anticipate questions, problems, hurdles, and stumbling blocks, and be prepared to respond (not react). What is the context? What are unseen concerns? What are red flags?

Expectation—The incoming runner expects the outgoing runner to be ready to receive the baton. The outgoing runner expects the baton to be placed properly with unmistakable timing and intentionality. What do supervisors expect from all parties involved, both pastors and the church leaders? Has this expectation been agreed upon and *communicated* to all appropriate persons?

Communication—Relay-race communication isn't rambling or simply "well intentioned." For instance, not "Hey, I'm getting closer. Are you ready?" but rather clear and focused communication so the speaker and receiver of the message are speaking the same language with the same urgency. The relay team communicates clearly: "Go! Go! Go!" and "Stick! Stick! Stick!" As Patrick Lencioni demonstrates in *The Advantage*, "Most teams communicate poorly because they haven't clarified sufficiently." Clarify, clarify, clarify the situation, expectations, and strategies, *then* communicate clearly! [2] Communication, as lifted up by Tom Mullins in *Passing the Leadership Baton*, also helps move the congregation "from uncertainty to anticipation." [3]

Execution—As with any team in any sport, regardless of the quality of preparation, there finally has to be execution that delivers results. Good execution in the Changeover Zone seldom happens without *personal* accountability. And creating a culture of accountability rests on the shoulders of the entire team individually and as a group.

Remember, as Michael Watkins insists, the reason to work so hard to have a good handoff isn't to brag that it was smooth and seamless; it is to accelerate the organization's performance. [4] In the church this means health and vitality, mission and ministry, growth and passion. It is to increase impact! This is the bottom line measure for a successful handoff.

Most coaches gauge the success of their runner's handoff through a metric measured with a stopwatch: hopefully, in a standard relay race the total time *in* the Changeover Zone of all four zones combined should *never exceed* the time it takes to run any one leg of race.

That is, coaches have mapped out what success looks like for the team during the transition. They give it a goal. Successful pastoral transitions also map out what success looks like in the Changeover Zone. Whatever the goal—loss of no members, conflict resolution, healing accelerated growth, or a myriad of other ones—all parties hold each other accountable to the question, What does success look like?

Success may well be different for every transition, but it is critical that supervisors and leaders define what it looks like in any given situation and communicate their understanding to all parties. This is what creates a culture of accountability.

What happens when the baton drops? This is where personal accountability becomes paramount. If a baton drops in a relay, the runner who last touched it is the only runner allowed to pick it up, and then only in the team's assigned lane. Usually if a baton is dropped, by the time a racer stops and picks it up the race is over, for all intents and purposes. There is little chance for the team to catch up. But teams still practice this drill of picking up a dropped baton *to instill a culture of personal accountability.*

What happens when a baton is dropped in the Changeover Zone of any given pastoral transition? Are the responsible parties willing to accept accountability and pick it up, or do they blame someone else? Are they willing to stoop to pick up the baton and not expect someone else to do it or blame someone else for it? Is there enough humility, openness, and trust to learn from the experience to sharpen the culture of accountability for the future? Going into the transition with open, upfront, honest conversation about personal accountability should a baton be dropped will help bring about a culture of accountability.

Those interested in creating a culture of accountability gather specific feedback on each pastoral transition. Examples of the kinds of questions asked:

- How is Average Worship Attendance today, compared to the date of the transition? Compared to one year ago?

- What was the percentage of loss, in terms of members/attenders leaving due to the transition?

- How does key leadership (lay and clergy) assess the transition—three months, six months, nine months, twelve months—after the change of pastors?

- Supervisors, inquire specifically about how your job performance is perceived by the church, exiting pastors, and arriving pastors. Assess the church's performance of its roles during the transition.

An organization committed to a culture of accountability places a premium on the time invested in gathering specific information, knowing full well that it will improve its overall stature and success. Organizations committed to accountability embrace the notion that mistakes will be made—the key is to make them worth making! A culture of accountability values what's learned from mistakes and redeems them, becoming better because of them, and leveraging them by teaching others the learnings.

Brief or superficial evaluations only serve to contribute to poor selection and little or no accountability. In fact, unredeemed mistakes lead to wasted opportunities, wasted time, and wasted effort.

Track coaches say their most important function as a coach is to listen to their runners and get feedback after every race: Condition of the track; what happened in each changeover; did someone loose acceleration, and if so, why? That is, they hold themselves accountable, debriefing and assessing everything right after the race, so they can be better prepared for the next race. This culture of accountability is paramount to the long-term success of the team.

In the words of Manteo Mitchell, "You don't want to let anyone down."

FOLLOWING A FOUNDING PASTOR

Being a second pastor is perhaps as challenging as planting a church.
Done well, the church will thrive; done poorly and there's likely no third
pastor coming.
—Lewis Center Study of Second Pastors survey respondent

The headline in the sports section of the Dallas Morning News blared out: "Handoff hiccup costs U.S." The story was about the women's 4 X 400 relay team coming in second to Jamaica by a scant 0.31 seconds, and stated it clearly, "the U.S. handoff wasn't clean, opening the door for the Jamaicans to win a close race."

The explanation portrayed in vivid detail the very small margin of error in a relay race: "When McCorory reached back with her left hand to receive the baton from Felix for the anchor leg, she grabbed air. That forced McCorory to pause ever-so-slightly to grab the stick on the second swipe. The whole thing took less than a second, but the race decided by 0.32 of a second."

Because the margin of error in the handoff from a founding pastor to the second pastor is so fragile, this section goes in depth to address the critical issues and provide solutions for the church, supervisors, and pastors involved.

Chapter 8

When a Church Goes through Its First Pastoral Change

Gold medals aren't really made of gold. They're made of sweat, determination, and a hard-to-find alloy called guts.

—Dan Grable

The bride turned around and instructed all the guests, "Now, everyone please go outdoors to the amphitheater; you will receive a small box, but please do not open it until the wedding party joins you." I had just blessed the marriage, and the wedding ceremony itself had ended. Like everyone else, I was curious as to what the bride had in mind.

Within minutes we were all positioned in the beautiful amphitheater carved into the base of the small hillside outside the lower level of the sanctuary building, each of us clutching a small flat box. "Now," said the bride, "open your box!"

Out of each box fluttered a living Monarch butterfly! It was beautiful as some two hundred butterflies exited their boxes and swirled about, instinctively shaping into a spiral as they gracefully fluttered upward toward the top of the amphitheater.

An audible, "Ahhhhhh" came from the assembled guests. No doubt in each of our minds were unspoken words like "dreams," "future," "hope," "joy," and "possibilities."

But as the butterflies rose to the top of the amphitheater, they caught the attention of the two hundred grackles nesting in the Bradford pear trees. In one motion the birds swooped in, attacking the butterflies just a few feet above us.

Almost instantaneously you could hear the "Ahhhhhs" turn into "Uuuuuughs!"

When a new church is planted, it is a thing of beauty, holding dreams, future, hope, joy, and possibilities. But it is startling how fast the "ahhhhhs" of hope turn to "uuuuuuughs" of disgust when things don't go as hoped. And a new church is never as vulnerable as when it goes through its first pastoral transition. Church leaders all over the country report tragic situations in which the dreams of the new church come crashing down when the founder leaves and a new pastor arrives. Frequently the crash happens faster than anyone could have imagined.

The main reason most people connect with a new church start is because they love the founder. For many, their experience in this new, exciting, spiritual venture represents their first exposure to a faith community as adults. They have invested time, energy, and money in being a part of something that has changed them and that they believed would change the world. Many participants, new or renewed to the faith, can't imagine church without the only pastor they've known.

In the best of circumstances, this transition will cause high anxiety. Done poorly, the transition can create paranoia and become toxic. Whatever the age of the new church start (although the younger it is, the more vulnerable) or the reasons for the change of pastors, the church is at risk.

The main risk factors can be categorized as follows:

Financial Investment Is at Risk

In most denominational new church starts, somewhere in the neighborhood of a quarter to half million dollars will be invested in the new church over forty-eight months. Funding comes in many ways, among them, the sale of older church properties and capital campaigns designed to underwrite a church-planting initiative.

Sometimes another fifty thousand to one hundred thousand dollars might come from the "mother church" that is birthing the new daughter congregation or extension campus, which also serves as its home base and sponsor. Every church has a tight budget, and this amount usually represents difficult debate within church leadership over priorities, raising such questions as, Does this make sense? Throughout the birthing process and the launch of the new church or campus, skeptics will monitor what happens to "their money."

From the first time the new church start begins to meet (even in planning meetings to grow the launch team) participants begin to learn stewardship by giving regularly. Even a relatively small group of people who make up the launch team will give generously of time and money. As the new church begins to have preview services, then regular worship, financial contributions and systematic giving may well generate in the neighborhood of another one hundred thousand dollars over the first forty-eight months. The church planter often will solicit family members and friends to support the new work, treating it as a mission project. Due to the passion of the planter and participants these "outside investors" are moved to generosity.

Needless to say, with all this financial investment, the transition must be done with great care and intentionality. If not, the new church often does not survive, and all that financial investment is gone.

Trust Development Is at Risk

If the young church is part of a wider band of churches or within a denomination, then the organization's trust is at risk. Many of the people coming to a new church have little or no prior contact with the "tribe" supporting the new church. And so, they're not as familiar with the tribe's selection process. Because many of the new members come from corporate or business or educational professions, they assume that the hiring process is similar to the organization that employs them. They understand some of the need for closed door meetings, but when decisions are made behind closed doors, the baton is dropped, And, because of a poorly conceived and executed pastoral transition, is it any wonder that the following comments are directed at the system: "Is this for real?" "Is this how you do business?" "We're outta here."

People's trust in the church is at risk—not just their local church, but the church at large. If people feel discounted, burned, and ignored, it often reinforces previous opinions and stereotypes. If they perceive the transition was implemented poorly and feel as though they've been duped into supporting what they now believe to be an inept system, they're much more likely to walk away from religious participation altogether.

Trust in each other is at risk. Even if church members tolerate the poorly implemented transition, and for whatever reason, agree to "hang in there and see it through," people often find themselves taking sides on a whole host of issues. Friendships can be stressed to the breaking point and relationships fractured. Divisions creep into the body over such things as: Who caused the founder to leave? Why didn't leaders tell us this, or why didn't they do that regarding the transition?

Real or imagined, these suspicions wander through the congregation. The incoming pastor suffers from these lingering emotions. Issues of loyalty and friendship are breeched. The stresses may cause people to behave badly toward one another, further decimating the trust level to the degree that it will be nearly impossible to regain momentum for the young church.

The Church Is at Risk

A young church is most vulnerable when going through its first pastoral transition, so its very existence is at risk. In a more established church a poorly performed handoff to an incoming pastor may not be fatal. The church is older and has begun to mature with staff and established systems in place. But when a botched handoff occurs in a church that's less than five years old and doesn't make sense to a critical mass of the people, or seems dishonoring of the pastor and/or the congregation, the results often times prove fatal.

Consequently, growth is at risk. There are thousands of churches in America that plateaued at less than 250 members, even though they are in growing communities. This is often due in large part to pastoral transitions that set the church back, instead of propelling it forward.

The discipleship of members is at risk. This is a sad collateral damage of poorly handled transitions. Participants in plateaued churches (in spite of being in growing mission fields) often are plateaued in their own discipleship and individual spiritual development. Transitions that are random, not well thought out, and carelessly executed cause skepticism and lack of buy-in on the part of members. So even when the disheartened church members stay in the church, they become victims of a general loss of intensity and passion on the part of the very church that is charged with helping them to grow spiritually. Consequently, they don't!

Even More, Souls Are at Risk

People have invested their time, energy, and resources in the new church. This investment *goes* somewhere—to the ministries of the church. And this investment *comes* from somewhere—a heart that has been touched, a life that has been impacted, a spiritual motivation that has been sparked. In short, this investment is a matter of the soul. For many in a new church, they have come to know Christ *through* their church and the Christian community they have experienced.

Consequently, but not coincidentally, people have formed their spiritual identity through their church. True, that identity is continually and constantly being shaped, but for some period of time when an individual has been involved in the new church, their life journey has intersected with their spiritual journey: it is a precious and formative time, not to be taken lightly.

While the world today is largely unchurched, those who have affiliated with a particular church have in fact connected their belief in God via their experience in the church. This is serious business! Especially new believers, who are often attracted to a new church, do not understand or comprehend the depth and breadth of God and theological underpinnings. But they believe, trusting that more will come clear as they mature and trusting more that God's loving nature will not let them down.

Not all that dissimilar from their belief in God is their belief in their church: they do not understand or are not even aware of the multiple nuances of the local church and its tribal arrangements with the "larger church beyond its walls," but they trust still that some system out there is looking out for them. A poorly conceived and implemented transition can shatter that trust in the church and often religious allegiance as well.

Even in the best-case pastoral transitions when a new church says "goodbye" to its founder and "hello" to its "second" pastor, there are unique dynamics at play. This can be seen in three areas: (1) authority, (2) pastoral perceptions, and (3) congregational involvement.

Because of these additional risk factors, supervisors are seeing the wisdom and benefits of starting the pastoral transition process—when the church enters the Changeover Zone—much sooner than a more-or-less "typical" pastoral change; thus stated: "The pastorate begins before the pastorate begins!"

First, consider the sense of authority. In a new church plant virtually everyone comes—and stays—because they like the pastor. They feel a deep personal connection with this amazing pioneer who birthed a church that seems wonderfully suited for them. People who don't like or connect with the founding pastor, usually don't stay. Consequently, the founder has a popular and inherent sense of authority within the congregation. The second pastor will not possess such authority; and the congregation will not buy into or follow their second pastor in the same manner they did with the founder. Nor can the second pastor simply fall back on the authority inherent in ordination and claim divine affirmation. True though it may be, seldom is it beneficial for the pastor to assert authority., Rather, the second pastor must win over the people and *earn* the right to authority. This takes time and intentionality.

Second, in a new church plant, unaware of ecclesiastical nuances, church members see and perceive *their* pastor as their "representative," almost in the priestly model as the pastor-mediator between themselves and God. They see their beloved pastor representing Christ to them in the hospital room during times of sickness and sadness; see their pastor representing them to God in times of family/marriage crises; see their pastor personally helping them navigate through tough times and times of joy, such as at the baptism of their baby. But in many ways, especially within denominational/ church networks, people are more likely to see the second pastor not as "their representative to God," but rather as "the tribe's representative to them." To ignore this, ignores the adversarial tone that quickly may arise from such an oversight. It's not uncommon to hear a comment such as, "They decide; we didn't ask and we didn't get a voice."

The third consideration has to do with how the early people become "involved" in a new church plant. From the opening days of the church most everybody gets involved and participate by virtue of being personally courted by the founder.

Folks are on the "take-down/set-up crew," or putting out yard signs, or volunteering in child care, or at the park for the community relay race, handing out bottles of water with the new church's name on it, or placing door hangers with church information around the neighborhood. That is to say, the newer the new church plant, the more likely that most people are "producers" of the church's ministry, not simply "consumers" of it.

But, as is typical in church life, the older the church gets, the more likely that "producers" can drift and default to become "consumers." It is typical for this gap between consumer-producer to drift wider and wider as the church ages. This "Producer-Consumer Gap Drift" is a reality that refers to the time it takes to get the first-time attender (consumer) to become actively involved (producer). The ability to turn consumers into producers is crucial for any growing church. The natural "drift" from the new church's "producer" culture to a "consumer" culture has generally fully set in by the time the new church goes through its first pastoral transition.

The founding pastor governs the gap between consumer/producer usually on the basis of his or her personality and leadership. The second pastor must develop systems to govern the gap, that is, those clearly designed, communicated, and accountable ways to (a) reach new people, (b) involve more people, and (c) help people grow in their relationships and discipleship.

The founder's function was to get people. And then get more people. And then get some more people. The second pastor must develop systems that *get people to get more people.* Systems should not be seen as the machinery of the church but as ways to accelerate growth. It's always about growth! To close the "consumer/producer gap," the second pastor can no longer rely solely on personally recruiting people. Rather, the second pastor must intentionally develop a new culture in which systems are not seen as bureaucracy but rather as life-giving pathways to personal, spiritual, and congregational growth. Not an easy task!

Because the arrival of the young church's first "new pastor" brings about culture change, it is beneficial to begin the transition process much earlier and with much more intentionality than a more "typical pastoral transition," thus, "The pastorate begins before the pastorate begins!"

While there can never be a guarantee for a successful transition from a founder to a second pastor, odds of a successful change of pastors are increased when the supervising agency develops a specific protocol for transitions having to do with a second pastor following a founder.

This protocol includes: (1) Thorough ways to teach and escort the church through the time of transition, (2) Intentional guidance for the departing pastor to set the stage for a great transition, (3) Creative, lighthearted ways to introduce the incoming pastor prior to arrival, and (4) Clearly communicated techniques for the incoming pastor to learn the culture of the church and to get "on-boarded" with excellence.

From the time a young church (and to almost the same degree, a church that has had a long-tenured pastor) enters the Changeover Zone, it will begin to navigate through six anxiety-driven questions:

1. Why is our founder leaving?

2. What is happening?

3. How will it happen?

4. What will the next pastor be like?

5. What will happen to my church?

6. What does it mean for me and my family?

Such questions, poorly addressed or ignored altogether, will only exacerbate the anxiety of the members. If left unaddressed, the young church faces the very real prospect of a mass exodus of people. And they don't just

55

leave that particular church; they are likely to leave the tribe. Even more sadly, often these people simply "leave church."

The number one reason for poor transitions—which can lead to lethal consequences—in these types of church settings is that supervisors treat them "like any other pastoral transition." They are not. There is no "one size fits all" approach to developing a commonly understood, accepted, and communicated Changeover Zone protocol. Each sponsoring agency can significantly improve the odds of better pastoral transitions by developing a protocol specific to its unique culture and setting. Hopefully, the Changeover Zone principles in this book will prove helpful. At a minimum, our experience indicates the protocol should include specific steps to cover:

- Justifiable variations from typical "selection protocols" regarding all aspects of the pastoral change (selection, timing of announcements, and so on)

- Creating a pool of trained second pastors

- Equipping supervisors with appropriate assessment tools for pastoral selection

- Providing specific "Saying Goodbye; Saying Hello" training for the church as it goes through the transition

- Developing a team of church leaders to share confidence-building "trustimonials"

- Making coaching available for twelve to eighteen months

- Seeking the counsel of a third-party advisor to enhance the decision as to when to make a pastoral change and consider possible successors

There is much mileage to be gained when the supervisor can speak to an anxious meeting of new church leaders going through its first pastoral transition and say with confidence and authenticity: "We believe in you enough to make a significant investment in you. We are going to do some specific things we don't normally do when there's a pastoral change, because we know you'll never have this time in your history again—receiving your first new pastor. So we want to do everything we can to make this a great time in the life of the church. We are going to provide training and coaching for you as a congregation over the next several months as you go through this transition; we will provide special training for potential second pastors (or follow long-tenured pastors); we will assist your current pastor in introducing your new pastor in good, healthy ways; and we will make sure your new pastor is a good fit for this church and will come in and immediately begin to learn your culture and get to know you in very definitive ways. As you've just heard from a layperson in another church very much like yours, this is an anxious time, but it can be a time of renewed energy and growth."

Chapter 9

Preparing for the Handoff

The One Hundred Days before *the New Pastor Arrives*

*The road to the Olympics leads to no city, no country. It goes far beyond
New York or Moscow, ancient Greece or Nazi Germany. The road to the
Olympics leads—in the end—to the best within us.*

—Jesse Owens, *Jesse: A Spiritual Biography*

T here's no guarantee to an uneventful and successful handoff. But,
with intentional planning, a supervisor—in conjunction with the
church and pastors—can greatly increase the odds of one occurring. As track coaches implore, "Never let the baton slow down!" While
paying attention to each and every pastoral transition, new church starts
face a more daunting challenge. A helpful way to frame the handoff is to see
it in two parts: the first one hundred days *before* the new pastor arrives and
the first one hundred days *after* the new pastor begins.

Every church operates within some system of receiving a new pastor.
Whatever the respective system, pastors enter the Changeover Zone the
day they officially learn they will become the new pastor of a given church.
Even if the knowledge of the new assignment isn't public, the incoming
pastor doesn't hesitate to begin the process of preparing for the change
to come.

Similarly, the church enters the Changeover Zone the moment it learns
officially that the congregation is about to receive a new pastor.

In a relay race, each team places some kind of "marker" (usually a
piece of bright tape) a few strides in front of each changeover zone at each
curve of the track. The runner waiting in position to receive the baton looks
back over her shoulder watching for her teammate to reach the marker,

anticipating that the passing of the baton is getting ready to happen. She had better be ready.

Improving the Odds of a Successful Transition

Pastoral transitions—when something is getting ready to happen—can be seen in the following "markers" for all parties involved:

1. The Private Notification: Saying "Goodbye" Part I
2. The Public Announcement: Saying "Goodbye" Part II
3. Saying "Goodbye" to the Departing Pastor
4. Saying "Hello" to the Incoming Pastor
5. The Transition itself

Each of these markers signifies a sequence in the handoff and to mishandle the baton invites serious consequences. The race can be over before it has ever begun.

The Private Notification

Saying "Goodbye" Part I

The first marker in the sequence is that of private notification. This is when the pastor learns she/he is going to a new church; it is when the church leadership learns they are receiving a new pastor. It is when the potential of the new arrangement becomes real. Most often, the private notification will be cloaked in confidentiality, until there is agreement on when, how, and who will make the public announcement.

What Not to Do:

The new extension campus in a fast-growing suburb had just celebrated its third year and had grown to a respectable size. A dedicated core leadership group was intentional and enthusiastic about getting to know their neighbors in the community. This enthusiasm was generating higher-than-expected offerings.

Still, the senior pastor of the main campus wanted to make a pastoral change in the extension campus, so he informed the extension campus pastor of the change and then arranged for his placement elsewhere. The senior pastor then asked his "tribe's" supervisor to meet with the leadership to inform them of the impending change. The extension campus pastor also was prepped and invited to the meeting.

An impromptu meeting was called and leaders from both campuses were summoned. They sat around the table, visiting and dressed casually, not knowing the details of the meeting. In walked the supervisor, attired in a dark suit. Without introductions or conversation he said: "You've been asked to this meeting so I could tell you that last night, I presented your pastor as the new pastor of another church. When we have selected your next pastor, I will let you know." He looked up at the stunned faces and asked pointedly, "Any questions?"

Silence. Finally one individual asked, "Do we have any say in this?" "Not really," replied the supervisor. "That's not the way we do it." He paused briefly and then said, "If there are no other questions, I'll let your pastor say a few words." On cue, their beloved pastor chimed in: "This is a great opportunity for me; I was surprised when they asked me about going to this other church, but as a pastor, I go where I am sent. I will sure miss you, but I'm also sure they'll find a new pastor that you will love like you've loved me."

Quickly the supervisor drew the fifteen-minute meeting to an end. People filed out in silence, many of them never to return to the church.

The lesson here for supervisors: avoid treating the private notification of the pastor leaving as perhaps the more typical protocol when an older established church faces a pastoral change. In a young church, people simply do not know or appreciate the tribal polity. Even if they did, such an abrupt approach shakes the foundation of confidence and trust.

Supervisors go a long way toward improving the odds of success if they have previously and intentionally built trust and rapport with any young and fledgling congregation. Here are three ways to help in that effort:

First, at the risk of being stereotypical, those in ecclesiastical positions sometimes forget to whom they are speaking when they sit across from a group of people who are trying to function in volunteer leadership of a church. In multiple debriefs with church leaders following a pastoral transition, we frequently hear, "Then this guy in the suit comes in..."

Newer churches tend to adopt a less traditional, more casual style, extending to language, attire, and protocol. Attenders of these churches often dress in jeans not pants or skirts; and polo shirts, not fancy blouses or button-down collars; and drink coffee during the service. Successful supervisors/overseers carve out time to do such things as handing out water bottles in the park with the rest of the launch team; coming to a fellowship gathering after a worship service; and joining one of the mission/outreach events. This is a "high reward" investment of time. We are not talking regularly; just once or twice will leverage your time and impact immensely when there is official "business" to tend to later on.

One supervisor had gotten on the e-mail distribution list of the launch team. Excitement was building for their first effort of reaching out to the community—running a booth during an area 5K race. Preparing water bottles, handout literature, schedules—all were circulating amongst the revved-up launch team members.

For reasons later regretted and apologized for, the supervisor hit "reply to all" with this tart message: "Do not include me in these e-mails; I do not have time to read about everything you are doing." Launch team members spent their day in the park mumbling and grumbling about that message. The sense that they were a distraction to "the system" that didn't support them provided an easy excuse when the new church plant began to falter. They didn't trust in the supervisor's presence or attempts to help them, right up until the day they officially closed.

Second, there is great value in gathering "trustimonials," recruiting a person from a church who has recently gone through a similar transition to share what the church leaders faced and how they handled it.

I know what you are feeling. A year ago our founding pastor left. Not only did he start the church, but he baptized my first baby. He is the only pastor my family had ever known. We were crushed and couldn't understand it. But you know, we've already come to love our new pastor! And we've actually noted gifts that our founder didn't have. My church is actually doing much better because it is built upon the great work of our founder and now being cared for by a new pastor who is also wonderful. It took some getting used to—hearing a different voice, seeing a different face, learning a different leadership style—but it has been such fun and so worth it!

This kind of "trustimonial" gains everyone's attention and trust. The listening group thinks, "Here too is a person from a church who has had a similar experience." Here is a person with credibility. The anxious crowd now sees a new friend with whom they could connect; someone just like them. Imagine how such a "trustimonial" dissipates fear, tension, anger, and angst now replaced with questions, excitement, and anticipation. "Trustimonials" trump most words from the professional supervisor.

Because a young church especially reaches those outside the church, the "trustimonial" approach affords the opportunity for supervisors to invite these members to participate in helping a church face similar challenges.

Such a process validates the experiences of these newer members and puts them in positions to help a sister congregation.

Third, like a proud parent, successful supervisors brag about new churches birthed on their watch! They lift up these babies to colleagues and anyone else who will listen. These supervisors carry plenty of congregational life photos in their phone. When they are speaking at some other church under their purview, they arrange to show at least one photo of the nearby new church on the screens, simply so they can brag on it: "Take a look at this picture; great things are happening at our new church. Please keep them in your prayers. Maybe even some of you can drop by for support once in a while." Do the same with casual hallway conversations: whip out that phone and show a baby picture to the person you are talking to. Brag on it!

People talk, and sooner or later, a person from some other church will talk to someone at the new church and share how excitedly the supervisor is talking about them. This earns trust! Then, when the supervisor has to play the part of supervising—even in a tough situation—trust has been earned. Sadly, often supervisors are perceived within a new church as a stranger—or even worse, as the sheriff.

Other conversations that fall under "private notification" are the ones occurring between the departing pastor and spouse, family, and key church leaders. While each tribe has specific boundaries around these conversations, the following protocol has proved very beneficial:

For many reasons confidentiality governs those specific persons with whom the departing pastor will speak and choose to handle the sensitive information during the "private" phase of the decision. Departing pastors cannot shirk this role of informing and honestly explaining their role and decision in the pastoral change. The moment the departing pastor begins to notify others marks the beginning of the Changeover Zone and will set the tone for what transpires.

Due to working relationships and friendships, there are some people within the departing pastor's world that deserve the courtesy of a private and confidential conversation. The departing pastor should make a short list of people with whom to share the news personally. To treat all people equally belies the relationship that the departing pastor has developed with certain individuals within the church. For them to hear news of their pastor's/ friend's/colleague's departure first in some large-scale public manor does not take into account their relational bonding.

Many successful departing pastors have spent the last four to six weeks of their active ministry with these kinds of meetings. At appropriate times, the pastor's spouse participates.

The Public Announcement

Saying Goodbye Part II

By the time the news is being made public, the departing pastor is well into the Changeover Zone. There is no set way to make the public announcement(s), but there are some good questions to be clarified before announcements are made: (1) What will be the impact of how announcements are made? (2) How and in what settings will people best process the announcement? (3) How will announcements be coordinated between the churches involved? Remember, often times while one church is saying "hello" to their new pastor, another church is saying "goodbye" to that same pastor. Coordination regarding pastoral changes must be done with genuine sensitivity that honors tribal polity and protocols.

The impact of the announcement is highly influenced by the *context* of the transition:

- Is the departing pastor retiring? Leaving on good terms? Still on site, or already gone?

- If already gone, is there a plan for the interim time?

- Is the incoming pastor an associate on staff or a former staff member who has been groomed to move into the senior role?

- Are there difficult or unresolved issues lingering in the background, such as urgent budget crisis, need to change worship venue, staff misbehavior, and the like?

- Is there a discernible pattern of dysfunction on the part of the church or clergy involved?

Often in younger churches the unwritten protocol surrounding a pastor or staff member leaving mirrors social norms: "It's bad form to break up through text," said one newer church lay leader. "Own up, and break up eye to eye." This may or may not be right in terms of a guiding principle, but in reality it is hard to do in a congregational setting. The problem: not everyone hears the same information at the same time. Subsequently, they spread their filtered information in a way that may not be accurate and can even be detrimental.

Our experience is that any announcement of any kind of major impact should be done by e-mail, so that people have a chance to process the information in their home, not surrounded by fellow congregants in a worship service or meeting.

Social media and our media-conscious worldview today not only facilitates but makes it almost imperative to provide real-time, accurate, instantaneous information regarding the announcement of a pastoral change. Below would be the sequential steps we see most often practiced in the most helpful way:

Notification. This is usually private, confidential, and shared by the departing pastor and supervisor with key leadership in a meeting setting. Often the departing pastor will choose to share this information—immediately prior to the formal meeting—personally by phone or face-to-face with key staff (if they are considered trustworthy of this still confidential information). The pastor may also alert a few laity who have become close friends and confidants.

Going Public. Announcements usually done in a public, coordinated setting, as follows:

1. For purposes stated earlier the departing pastor must stay focused but also let the designated lay spokesperson handle much of the public news role. The departing pastor would be well served to stay out of the spotlight with these announcements. The tendency is to try to "soften" the impact, which may cause the departing pastor to say or promise something that's not appropriate or may harm the handoff.

2. Both departing pastor and designated congregational leader/ chair of personnel committee compose a written communiqué (approved by appropriate leaders) via email and/or postal, announcing the change and detailing the specifics (those that are known at this time). This should be done the first day of the week (if by mail, the letters should be mailed Saturday night), the email would be sent on Monday, so that the vast majority of the congregation receives the news early in the week. The communique affirms the change, the departing pastor confirms the fact during the upcoming Sunday

worship, and the congregational leader will share similar news. *Note: Should the decision be to make the announcement publicly during a worship service setting prior to a letter (strongly discouraged), be sure that a more detailed e-mail goes out immediately following the worship service. This allows people who were not in attendance to learn the same information at about the same time and limits the likelihood that someone who attended worship will give their own version of the announcement that may be off-target.*

3. Posting the news on Facebook the same day as the e-mail, and the use of other social media as appropriate.

4. In this day of social media, the need for updates is increasingly important. Someone should be assigned to update the congregation as things transpire in real time.

5. Pastor and key lay leader share together during worship about the impending change, following up on e-mail and social media posts.

6. Following the announcement, it is strongly encouraged that the departing pastor, spouse, and church leaders refrain from taking phone calls from curious church members. All statements should focus on the public and posted updates available to all. Far too often, taking calls from inquiring minds, no matter how innocent they appear, leads to botched transfers of the baton.

7. In the remaining weeks of the active ministry, the departing pastor continues to interpret the change in a powerful, healthy way to the congregation via sermons, blogs, newsletter articles, meetings, and so forth.

8. As soon as the successor is made public, the departing pastor will begin to groom a relationship with the incoming pastor and take steps (as described in chapter 5) to visibly "pass the baton" and make introductions of the new pastor in endearing ways.

Introducing the Incoming Pastor: Saying "Hello"

The third marker in the Changeover Zone centers on the most visible part of the transition, which involves introducing the incoming pastor to the congregation in a public forum. Usually this introduction occurs during the scheduled worship service (typically by video) and precedes the new pastor's arrival to the church, sometimes months in advance.

Introductions should follow this pattern: (1) As scheduled, make the public announcement during the worship service(s) regarding news of a new pastor, accompanied by introductions with biography and résumé. (2) Use other media the following week with similar information. (3) Outline a schedule of ongoing introductions of the incoming pastor and family that are creative, compelling, and momentum-building. To outline the schedule start with the actual "first Sunday beginning date" and work backward, scheduling a minimum of six to eight public weeks in which to introduce the new pastor via videos, photographs, and/or other creative ways. (4) Begin to do the planning—in advance of the arrival of the new pastor—for a "listening tour," which the incoming pastor will execute during the first one hundred days on the job.

Some suggestions for the departing pastor and planning team:

1. Ask the incoming pastor to send three sets of five fun facts that will enthrall the congregation. For instance:

   - I grew up on a farm.
   - I've been to the Holy Land six times.
   - I love to wear cowboy boots.
   - My husband has caught four foul balls at Rangers Stadium.
   - I live and die on Nebraska Cornhusker football.
   - I grew up collecting Santa Clauses.

2. For three weeks play the game by distributing index cards that include at least one of the five fun facts, but hide each of the facts in multiple choice options made up by the planning team. Example:

   - I love pistachio ice cream.
   - My favorite game as a kid was hide and seek.
   - I grew up collecting Santa Clauses.
   - I secretly covet an Oakland Raiders bobble head.

66

The departing pastor puts on the "game show" host hat and then invites the congregation to circle the facts they guess to be true. As each fact is revealed this affords the departing pastor every opportunity to endear the incoming pastor to the congregation. With each fact revealed, a different fun photo of the new pastor can be displayed on the screen.

The one hundred (or so) days leading up to a change of pastors are often overlooked or taken casually. The result usually hurts the handoff and makes it harder on the new pastor and her or his family. We hope we've made a case for being intentional and for all parties involved to allow for this important "marker moment" time in the life of the church. We have shared some best practices that we've seen work extremely well in a local church when saying "goodbye" and preparing to say "hello" during a pastoral change. Hopefully these practices will stimulate new ideas for having a great transition that will enable the church to burst out of the Changeover Zone into its future!

COACHING TIP: Wherever possible, avoid the incoming pastor being introduced to the congregation through church meetings and "business" prior to arriving as pastor. Somewhere in the meeting the pastor will be asked to weigh in on business without having any real understanding of the church's context or culture. No matter how the pastor responds, some people may not like her or his approach, which can lead to negative impressions of the new pastor with long-lasting consequences.

Chapter 10

Receiving the Handoff

The First One Hundred Days after *the New Pastor Arrives*

Joining a new company is akin to an organ transplant—and you are the new organ.

—Michael Watkins

In his book *The First 90 Days*, business author Michael Watkins introduces his readers to the challenges a leader faces when moving from one company to another. The incoming leader has to learn the culture, nuances, practices, politics, and habits of the new company; all in the first ninety days. Watkins calls this "onboarding."

In the Changeover Zone, the same act is described as "receiving the baton and charging ahead." All in the first one hundred days.

While theoretically there's no such thing as a pure comparison, practically speaking most transitions follow a common path. A pastor, for instance, moving from one United Methodist congregation to another is still working in the same organization, albeit in a different location. Theoretically this is true, but practically speaking, moving from one church to another church necessitates "onboarding" behaviors and practices. The incoming pastor/leader must work to earn trust and respect, discern the church's cultural nuances and practices, discern it's ministry and mission, as well as build relationships with the key people who make ministry happen.

Incoming pastors get this. They know that the people in their new church know more about their church than the collective wisdom of outsiders. They take great precautions to position themselves as "learners." Some supervisors think the church should wait a year to get to know the pastor before entering into this shared learning time. But that is like getting the cart before the horse. *Doing* the work is what builds the relationships, trust,

68

and respect that allow the church to get to know the pastor and the pastor to get to know the church.

The steps to take in the Changeover Zone may vary. There is no exhaustive checklist, but the following practices help position the incoming pastor for early success.

Conducting a Listening Tour

The first step in the sequence of receiving the handoff is to conduct a "listening tour" during the first one hundred days to learn the culture of the church and to begin to build new relationships. This onboarding tool is based on the need for the arriving pastor to learn the congregation's culture, context, history, and people. The listening tour provides a great way to do this.

The listening tour is typically a series of casual meetings, such as sharing dessert, in homes of congregants. A key member or family in the church would host a group of people in their home. (Small groupings of 5-15 are most advisable as everyone will want to participate in the conversation.) The idea is to get each existing group in the church, and every individual not currently in a group, to be able to come together to meet the new pastor and to share their perspective on the church. While the best venues for the listening tour will be in homes, sometimes this is not possible. Only after exhausting other neutral sites should the church facility itself be used.

The listening tour works best when *organized* by the departing pastor and *setup* by the church leaders prior to the new pastor's arrival. During the Changeover Zone the departing pastor and church leaders take responsibility to (a) solicit the host homes; (b) create the groupings, based on existing groups or on some other criteria such as geography, age-range, common affinity, or simply convenience of schedule; (c) arrange for staff or volunteers to send out publicity and invitations, which include an RSVP system; and (d) have the schedule completed and ready to hand off to the incoming pastor.

The departing pastor, already familiar with the social and ministry groupings, personality conflicts, and culture is best suited to organize the listening tour. In counsel with the church leaders, the schedule is finalized. While sometimes it happens and proves to be okay, to ask the incoming pastor to organize the listening tour exposes the process to unnecessary landmines, leading to numerous pastoral faux pas that are not easily dismissed or forgotten.

The incoming pastor visibly accepts the baton by then *conducting* the listening tour. Neither the supervisor nor the departing pastor participates in the actual listening tour. The incoming pastor is now taking the leadership role in the church.

The incoming pastor then arranges for a church leader to serve as an "escort" for each event. The escort brings great value in two ways: first, driving the pastor to each designated location, and second, serving as the acknowledged note-taker during the listening tour. The first function takes pressure off the brand-new pastor to find the address in a strange community; the second allows the pastor to be totally "present" with people, make eye contact, and focus on relationship building. Often, the drive home following the event provides strategic moments for debriefing and relationship building with someone from the church leadership.

The reason there needs to be a designated note-taker is because at the listening tour session—after enjoying dessert and appropriate introductions—the pastor will provide participants with a 3x5 card in which they are instructed to write down their answers to three questions:

1. What is one thing I need to know about this church?

2. What is one way that we are going to reach new people?

3. What is one dream you have for our church?

Some churches add two additional questions:

4. What is one thing you are afraid I might do?

5. What is one question you would like to ask me?

Note that question number one references "this church," not yet expressing "ownership" by the new pastor; question number two references "we," now expressing ownership and partnership, and clearly lets folks know that the agenda is "reaching new people." It's important for the incoming pastor to state from the beginning that a significant part of a church's purpose is to reach new people; and Question three references "our church," expressing full ownership, partnership, and teamwork.

Allow a few minutes for people to think about (or even briefly record on the card) their answers while enjoying dessert. Then go around the room and allow people to introduce themselves and share their answers, one question at a time. Make sure this is pressure free—honor those who are not wired to share publicly. (Invite them to share with you later in some other way.) Some pastors collect the cards at the end of the session; others rely on the note taking.

Some pastors prefer to ask participants to write down answers to the questions prior to the gatherings. This allows everyone time to consider what they would like to communicate about their church and discourages anyone from going off on a rant during the meeting.

Other than general questions, wise incoming pastors resist the temptation to answer questions from the group regarding church matters, business, the latest giving figures, and so forth. The purpose of the listening tour is to "listen," not expostulate or give a "state of the church" speech.

During the first hundred days, it is key that the incoming pastor sprinkles "this is what I heard during the listening tour" into sermons, announcements, meetings, and other public gatherings. The idea isn't to quote individual respondents (although that might be helpful with appropriate permission) but to demonstrate that the incoming pastor has listened intently to the people, and the exercise wasn't a waste of time. This builds trust and credibility.

"Why We Joined" Feedback

The second tool at the incoming pastor's disposal is the "Why We Joined" form (see appendix). It will reveal useful and actionable information about each person without resistance and without disrupting any existing "this is the way we've always done it" barriers. This form is dispersed to those people in the church who have been attending or joined within the last twelve months. (Some churches change the form to "Why We Are Attending.") It allows the new pastor to learn from the "newer" people and begin to discern patterns that will propel the church further forward in its mission. One of the questions asked, "Who or what influenced you to join?" affords the incoming pastor to provide immediate affirmation. For example, if the name of a particular person is listed, then the new pastor can send a photocopy with a note to that particular person with generous praise.

Regardless of the scope of use, most churches send this one-page form—because it is soliciting such valuable information—as a separate mailing (either first class, e-mail, SurveyMonkey, or some other way). It is not buried in some "new member packet" kind of communication.

But the main reason for the "Why We Joined" form is that it diffuses many conflicts and stubborn obstacles at leadership meetings. As the forms arrive and are collected, the incoming pastor disseminates copies randomly for committee members to peruse at any given meeting. Quickly they begin to learn what the new people are saying and feeling.

"Way to Go!" Notes

The third tool yields exponential results. It is the organized, intentional practice of sending "Way to Go!" notes.

Most incoming pastors find the note-sending (or digital) initiative to be most helpful when they recruit (yes, right from the beginning) an ad hoc group of church veterans to meet at the church midweek for the purpose of identifying persons to receive that week's notes.

First, the group carefully peruses all community newspapers serving the area community around the church. (Some communities will have multiple regional or neighborhood papers; some will have only one; some will have none but will rely instead on a larger metropolitan paper servicing its town. This activity is fun and conversational; and it builds relationships! When someone in the group recognizes the name of someone they know to be part of the church, they will: (a) highlight the person's name, (b) clip out the article or news announcement, and (c) include it in the envelope to send to the person with the pastor's brief, handwritten note scrawled on personal stationary letterhead that reads, "Way to go!" Short, sweet, and to the point. That's all. No need for lengthy notes. Just a short, simple "Way to go!" (or a similar sentiment that matches the pastor's personality). Have the assembled group members or administrative staffing address the envelope.

This note may be sent to a well-known church member who has just been announced as the head of a major charity in your community. Or, it may be sent to an eighth grader whose name appears on the academic honor roll at her middle school that is printed in the community paper. It makes no difference. People love to be recognized and they will appreciate receiving a personal note from their pastor. As a bonus: people who receive a "Way to Go!" note will likely tell someone else about it. This approach can of course be modified to meet the growing news media outlets that are digital rather than print.

Additionally, this process opens up the door to reach new people. If a member of the "Way to Go!" team recognizes the name of someone in the community who has done something newsworthy or admirable, a "Way to Go!" note affords the opportunity for the new pastor to reach beyond the church's four walls. This act reinforces the value of reaching new people.

Separately, "Way to Go!" notes can be directed toward specific staff members. Often these people are overlooked in all the noise of the new pastor's arrival. The incoming pastor who pays attention to small, often overlooked acts by staff members can utilize "Way to Go!" notes to build morale and raise energy.

This tool helps create a culture of attentiveness, affirmation, and appreciation that will undoubtedly begin to spread throughout the congregation.

In addition to using these three onboarding tools, an incoming pastor must avoid the following three pitfalls: (1) overlooking staff, (2) casting vision too soon, and (3) undervaluing the importance of learning together.

Staff and Church Leader Introductions and Events

Successful incoming pastors set aside significant time during the first hundred days to meet and build relationships with all ministry staff and strategic church leaders. The staff, paid and unpaid, have been impacted significantly during the pastoral transition. Having a new "boss" raises anyone's anxiety. Incoming pastors plan fun, casual, social times to reduce this stress. The time for evaluation and performance reviews happens much later. In all manner of settings: homes, restaurants, coffee shops, sporting events, movies, and so on, the incoming pastor visibly gives credit, acknowledges hard work, and expresses appreciation to various staff and leaders. Honoring these important people is a sure way to build morale and gain trust for the work going forward.

Casting Vision Too Soon

Soon after—and sometimes even before—an incoming pastor arrives, the question is asked, "What is your vision for our church?" Be cautious. Vision casting can and should be a fruitful part of the onboarding process, and if done correctly can solidify your pastorate and allow you to be accepted more quickly as the church's new leader. There is a sequential path to vision casting that leads to success in the onboarding process:

- First, cast THEIR vision.
- Second, cast A vision.
- Third, cast YOUR vision.

Getting the sequence out of order likely will lead to barriers, resistance, and in some cases the end of your ministry before it really gets started. Many overly eager pastors new to a church inadvertently discount their predecessors and the congregation by immediately casting some new, triumphant vision, before they've gotten to know the people. Different people, at different times, will react to this perceived affront in different ways—some immediately, others will let it fester for weeks, months, or even years. But sooner or later it will fester and then explode. Remember that axiom of the pastor's relationship to the congregation: "If as a pastor you love your people more than you stretch them, you will soon be known as their chaplain; if you stretch your people more than you love them, you will soon be known as their former pastor!"

The sequence may take weeks, months, or even years. The chronology is not as important as the sequence. First, get to know "their" vision, whether it is publicized and well known or simply an unstated part of congregational life; don't judge it, question it, or doubt it. Just cast it as a way of honoring the church and its past. Second, cast a specific vision within the church's larger vision. For instance, if the church's vision is "Meeting the needs of our neighbors," cast a vision and be the advocate for an initiative to collect two thousand pairs of shoes for the homeless. This will allow people to get used to the new pastor's voice as a vision caster that doesn't threaten or discount them. Then, finally, cast "your" vision, after you truly know the people, the context, and have let God speak to your heart.

Learning Together

Successful incoming pastors realize that no matter how smart they are or how much they know about "church," the people in their new church know more about *their* church than does the new pastor. They take great caution to not be perceived as a "solo-practitioner" or "lone wolf" looking at the church's future but as a partner in learning. So in addition to the three tools, we recommend that during the onboarding process the incoming pastor be intentional in involving others—staff and laity—in some kind of shared learning experience. Some supervisors think the church should wait a year to get to know the pastor before entering into this shared learning time. But that is like getting the cart before the horse. *Doing* the work is what builds the relationships, trust, and respect that allow the church to get to know the pastor and the pastor to get to know the church. Study something together; go through a focused, intentional long-term transformation process; be intentional!

Strategic Preaching

The Power of the Pulpit in the Changeover Zone

Running teaches us to challenge ourselves. It pushes us beyond where we thought we could go. It helps us find out what we are made of. This is what we do. This is what its all about.
—Pattisue Plummer, US Olympian

Pastor Duane walked into the church's pulpit for the very first time. He faced a congregation that had only recently said "goodbye" to their pastor of twenty-seven years. He began his sermon with these words, "My daddy used to tell me that the three hardest things in the world were (1) to climb a fence leaning toward you, (2) to kiss a girl leaning away from you, and (3) to preach your first sermon in your new church." The place erupted in laughter, and questioning looks immediately turned to accepting smiles.

Duane went on to thank the congregation for their gracious welcome, for helping him unpack boxes, and for making sure the church building was opened on time and everything ready to go on this, his first Sunday. He then went on to voice praise for the departed pastor. He demonstrated his awareness of the community and its history by referring to city landmarks, such as the school built by hardworking immigrants, three generations removed.

Using the church's video screen, he flashed photos of him holding his twin grandsons, and his wife standing next to him, peering into the window of the old school. Noting another familiar landmark in town, he added, "I can't wait till next week when I'm going to show you a picture of my little granddaughter climbing a tree in that orchard. That's when I'm going to preach about 'going out on a limb' as we look together at our future." Again, people chuckled at the pun and at his obvious grandfatherly, loving nature. Tension in the room evaporated.

Duane then said, "But this morning I want to share with you one of my favorite scriptures, Ephesians 3:20, because of something I heard at our first listening tour dessert last Wednesday night." On cue, the screen displayed a nice-looking invitation: "Haven't signed up for a listening tour dessert? See the schedule and reserve your space today!"

Duane, utilizing what he heard during his first listening tour, then said "This is what I heard from one of our members at the listening tour on Wednesday: 'One dream I have for our church is to be more like Jesus and find some ways to serve the children right here in the county.'" He paused and then stated, "You probably know before I became a preacher I was an elementary school principal, so you can see why I am so excited about becoming your new pastor."

Duane's story highlights two things with regard to preaching: (1) the incoming pastor already possesses communication skills and doesn't need training in that area, and (2) preaching in the Changeover Zone requires strategic planning and attention.

Regardless of who's sitting in the congregation during the first one hundred days, preaching affords the incoming pastor to make this impression: "Wow! I wasn't sure we had the right minister, but that sermon convinced me." Exactly the response Duane received!

Preaching offers the minister the singular opportunity to impress a broad range of people in a short period of time. In the first one hundred days of the church transition, the incoming pastor will begin to conduct listening tours and meet dozens of people, involving countless interactions. Then by giving thoughtful attention to answers gleaned from the listening tour cards, the incoming pastor organizes and references thoughts bolstered with, "This is what I heard in the listening tour." This public use of the listening tour demonstrates the incoming pastor's desire to listen and learn and embrace much of what the church is about.

Having everyone assembled together on a Sunday morning offers a different type of interaction: a one-way conversation, uninterrupted; the minister controls the topic and the content. This is the single greatest opportunity to begin to impact and influence the congregation.

During the first one hundred days it also means the minister has only a few times to make a "first" impression and recognizes the variety of people sitting in the audience. As with any congregation there are existing members who are either excited, skeptical, or withholding their opinion about the new pastor. Others in attendance will be those who have left the church in the recent past for a variety of reasons, but are now returning to give the new minister a chance. First-time guests will visit the church during this time;

some because they have heard from friends and community buzz that the church has a new minister; others will be there because of their own needs or desires and may not know anything about a change of pastors. And while the incoming minister can't fix everything in the first one hundred days, the pulpit provides an excellent platform from which to shape the culture and move the church out of the Changeover Zone.

Planning Sermons in the Changeover Zone

Strategic sermon planning begins way before the incoming pastor receives the baton or arrives at the new church. The incoming pastor has outlined the first one hundred days worth of sermons, (approximately three months), that is, intentionally planning out what messages to communicate and how. A successful strategic preaching plan maintains awareness of the calendar and propels the pastor to charge out of the Changeover Zone with baton in hand. To assist in the planning, see the seven strategic components listed below and incorporate them throughout the first three months:

1. Introduce yourself and your family in real-life vignettes.

2. Include humor as a way to get through resistance and anxiety.

3. Reveal your heart and passion.

4. Demonstrate your character, personality, and professionalism.

5. Share favorite scriptures and how you apply the Bible to daily life.

6. Lift up community history and values to connect with the congregation.

7. Indicate how much you care about your new church and are excited to be here.

Most clergy know they are making a change much sooner than one hundred days. In the case of some denominations, advance notice could be several months; in the case of others, it may occur with little or no warning.

Either way, sermon preparation can begin to happen easily and quickly before ever arriving at the new church.

Before ever arriving, the new pastor should evaluate the attendance patterns of that particular time of the year. Sure, there will be a few extra people the first few Sundays of the pastor's arrival, but the vast majority of church members don't alter their vacation plans to coincide with their new pastor's arrival. Consequently, the incoming pastor cannot rely on just the first few Sundays to make an impression. Thought must be given to include the above topics the first one hundred days of preaching.

When it comes to planning these sermons, many pastors arrive at their new church during an "off season," that is to say, the time in the calendar where much of the congregation is away on vacation. Those incoming pastors who take the first couple of Sundays to "download" their bio fail to take into account just how many (or how few) people will get a sense of their new pastor. Strategic preaching takes into account the necessity of the entire one hundred days.

Many a minister has expended significant sermon capital during times when a large percentage of the congregation is away on vacation or occupied in some other manner. In other words, good material fell on far fewer ears! Looking at a calendar will help the minister plan sermons accordingly.

Should the incoming pastor preach a series? It all depends. Does the series require the congregation to attend each and every Sunday to benefit? If so, good luck. Even during the course of the year, few people attend every Sunday. So, if a series is planned, each sermon will need to be designed and crafted to stand on its own merits and not rely on the previous sermon(s) to make sense. Consequently, individual sermons delivered skillfully should be the norm during the first one hundred days.

Reruns Acceptable

A mistake that many ministers make is to be tethered to the idea that only "original" sermons should be preached. During that first one hundred days, however, consider how such a misguided conviction robs the new pastor of valuable networking time and social interaction with the new congregation. Add to that the family demands of moving, getting settled, meeting people, learning the basics of the new church, and the emotional stress of just having said goodbye to a previous congregation—this is a tough time. To compound it, the new pastor attempts to give 100 percent to both "getting onboard" and "preaching a great message."

One or the other will suffer greatly. Either the sermon will soar to new heights, frequently over the heads of the people, who then may well say the pastor is "impersonal," or the sermon will suffer because the pastor's time was taken up with meetings. This does not need to happen during the critical first one hundred days.

Success in the Changeover Zone relies heavily on the personal interactions and the relational equity built in the first one hundred days. Consequently, most pastors have very little time for writing original sermons, much less planning a preaching calendar. The use of "reruns"—sermons that have been preached before that require few adjustments—can be prepared in a much shorter period of time, and yet delivered with conviction and certainty. Frankly, given the other demands during the Changeover Zone, pastors should spend as little time as possible creating new sermons, freeing up time to do those things discussed earlier in the book that are essential to success in the Changeover Zone. Some pastors have expressed anxiety over the fact that the sermon is not original. If it was worthy of being preached once, it's worthy of being preached again.

It is okay during the transition for pastors to gather their best ten to twelve "reruns" and spend time tweaking them to the proper context, making sure to build in the seven strategic components listed earlier in this chapter. If the sermon was good the first time it was preached, it will be that much better the second time.

Topics to Preach On during the First One Hundred Days

The use of the Bible stands at the center of every sermon to unfold the riches of God's grace found in Jesus Christ, and all pastors pray that the sermon delivers some sense of hope and opportunity for meaningful conversation to occur within the heart of each and every person in attendance.

However, opinions vary as to what topics the incoming pastor should address: from declaring theology beliefs or values, to setting the vision and direction of the church, to correcting theology and/or negative attitudes, the list goes on *ad infinitum.*

While the above topics need attention, and lots of it, incoming pastors are ill equipped to speak into the hearts of the congregation in the early days. Both the new pastor *and* the congregation are just getting acquainted. Remember, both pastor and congregation are going through an emotional and relational transition.

So the preaching goal in the first hundred days is to get off to a good start and move people to return the next Sunday. Often incoming pastors defer important topics and issues, including sermons regarding direction and vision, until after the listening tours are completed. To earn the right to speak on these things and others, incoming pastors must share the one thing everyone wants to see: their heart.

Until that first Sunday in the pulpit, many church members have not met their new minister. Not once! And if they have, probably only formally during the listening tour or some church leadership meeting. They may have only seen their minister from a distance and may never experience the minister any closer for some time. How then does the congregation come to know who their minister is? For example, congregations often say, "We know our minister believes 'X,' but we know little or nothing about our minister." Remarkably, some ministers have gone years in their church without ever referencing or revealing any of their background. Some congregations don't know where their minister grew up, number of siblings, interests, or hobbies. This does not bode well for the incoming pastor's ability to influence and lead a congregation; and though they are the church's "minister," they will rarely be referred to as "our pastor."

Using the pulpit allows new ministers, in a sense, to introduce themselves to their congregation: warts and all. This can be done systematically over the first one hundred days. Ministers can map out a plan to share some of who they are; not necessarily unbridled transparency, but rather a systematic unfolding of what made them who they are today. Their upbringing, their conversion story, their call into the ministry, their education, their life experiences, their family can be introduced in "snippets" all throughout the first one hundred days of sermons...and with plenty of pictures!

Instead of taking one Sunday to download all this biographical information, the new minister spreads this personal sharing over the first one hundred days. By taking several Sundays to do this, weaving in "vignettes" week after week, the pastor invites the church to see their minister as a human being, walking through life just as they are. This approach takes into account changing attendance patterns of today's churchgoers and recognizes that even a good loyal member may only be in the worship service sporadically to hear these biographic sketches unfold. If it is done in just one or two weeks, regulars may miss, and even more first-time attenders who will be coming to check out the new pastor.

Stories abound of successful incoming pastors who are diligent in using pictures to introduce themselves and their family. Often the new minister will visit local attractions, eateries, and so forth with their family, taking pictures and putting them on the screen. Selfies work wonders! The receiving congregation loves this. They like to know their new minister is settling in, enjoying what their community has to offer. Seeing these candid photos does much toward gaining followership in the Changeover Zone. The congregation wants to call their new minister "pastor." Stories of the heart help the congregation visit the minister's living room, which shortens the time frame and maximizes the impact.

One Item Every Sermon Must Have

As Duane demonstrated, topics aside, every sermon delivered in the first one hundred days must contain humor. Not necessarily side-splitting guffawing laughter, at least not in the early days. But, at a bare minimum, enough humor to have the entire congregation wanting to laugh. The Bible affirms this! Proverbs 17:22 says, "A joyful heart helps healing, but a broken spirit dries up the bones" (CEB), and Psalm 126:2 adds, "Our mouths were suddenly filled with laughter; our tongues were filled with joyful shouts" (CEB).

Ever since the announcement of their former pastor's departure, the church has amassed a number of emotions: shock, sadness, anxiety, fear, relief, and so on. When the church gathers on Sunday mornings, these emotions feed on each other. Now, they are gathering for the first times to meet and hear their new minister; and all assurances aside, they still retain their emotions. While the congregation may celebrate their previous pastor's ministry, underlying fears remain.

That's why the incoming minister needs to lead the church through the emotional uncertainty, and laughter more than anything else is the uniting emotion for any group.

Some ministers, rightly so, don't view themselves as comedians, but they wrongly assume this means they can't create laughter. Of course they can, and must. Beyond telling a joke on themselves or anyone else, any number of tools provide the minister the means to bring the congregation to laughter: video clips, pictures/images, stories downloaded from the Internet—all can provide ample amounts of humor. Even the most serious-minded minister can find these things.

Laughter is good for the heart, and group laughter is good for the group. Getting people to laugh together, week after week, may be the only thing people will remember from the first one hundred days. But laughter brings life and hope and begins to set the tone for other interactions the congregation will have with the incoming pastor. It also will shorten the time before people begin to let down their guard and use the term "our pastor."

In some cases, the congregation may not respond immediately. This only indicates their level of anxiety or sadness. Too many pastors have attempted interjecting humor once or twice and then dismissed the non-response with something like, "These people are just more serious-minded." Not at all! They are emotional beings. Perhaps they are sad, damaged, confused, uncertain, or just plain skeptical. Successful incoming pastors read the emotional thermostat of the congregation. Many pastors have reported it took weeks to get their new congregation to laugh together.

In the early days, maybe the congregation will only chuckle. Not to worry. This happens often. Keep at it; week after week inject some humor into the sermon. Let the people know that you like to laugh and that it's okay to laugh in church. As the chief shepherd of the church, the pastor must lead the congregation to the land of hope. It is a journey best navigated with joy, which often begins with laughter.

Consider the other components needed to accomplish strategic preaching in the first hundred days.

You "reveal your heart and passion" by saying it and showing it. Start with the heart—what and who and how do you love? What breaks your heart? What makes it soar? "Let your heart be glad," and let your folks know why.

Character, personality, and professionalism are demonstrated by how a pastor relates to people. Every worship experience offers the pastor a golden opportunity to express gratitude to someone or to groups of people; to clap for nursery workers, custodians, teachers, or others on the platform or in the background.

Sharing favorite verses from the Bible accompanied by vignettes from the pastor's life all serve to introduce the congregation to the spiritual life of the new pastor.

Lifting up community history and values in the sermon accomplishes two things: first, it teaches some fascinating community history that most people have overlooked and forgotten; and second, it shows that the incoming pastor is conducting field research. Both dynamics impress people—guests and veterans alike!

To succeed in a relay race the runner receiving the baton must charge out of the changeover zone at top speed. The runner trains for this handoff, sweats over every detail, prepares in a team mindset, and anticipates the moment. So it is with a pastoral transition, and preaching is the accelerator. Make it successful! Make it strategic!

What to Expect in the Changeover Zone

All It Takes Is All You've Got

The function of a leader within any institution: to provide that regulation through his or her non-anxious, self-defined presence.
—Edwin H. Friedman, *Failure of Nerve*

When charging out of the Changeover Zone what should the incoming pastor expect to accomplish in the first hundred days? The answer: Expect to meet some wonderful people, begin new friendships; see the church's potential and experience the exhaustion of being responsible for it all. And finally, expect that the situation is not as good nor as bad as presented.

Don't Panic! Some People Will Leave

In the most successful transitions, there will be people who will leave. In fact, pastoral transitions afford people who have been ambivalent about the church for some time the opportunity to depart. This is one of the toughest things for the incoming pastor and church leaders to accept.

Some of these people have been the backbone of the church; they are wonderful, strong, committed members. Other people will have had varying degrees of vested interest and years of involvement; some may even be dysfunctional or even toxic members. Regardless, when someone leaves, other members notice it and begin to talk about it and speculate and point fingers of blame...often at the new pastor. For the pastor, this is painful. It hurts. As one pastor said, "It's a kick in the gut!"

This is not the time for the new pastor and church leaders to panic. Concern over people's departures can overwhelm any meeting. Wise leaders expect this and defer such discussions to the sidebar conversations requiring further information.

The following is a list of the kinds of departures that occur during any pastoral transition:

Break Aways

This group has worked hard and been through a lot for a long time. They "just need a break." In all honesty, they've probably been looking for the right time to leave for some time. They had planned to leave regardless of how the transition was handled or who the new pastor was. For example, perhaps their teenager found new friends in another church's youth group, and the parents will do anything to keep their kid going to church, including transferring their membership. Or a divorce has come into someone's life situation and they need a fresh start that includes a different church family. Or they are just tired of meetings, activities in which their participation is expected, and they need a break and depart for a church where they can be more anonymous and just "enjoy going to church."

Pushed Aways

These people have been angered by the way the transition was handled, feeling that they were locked out of the decision making process.

Step Aways

This group stays through the transition but can't get over the reality that the new pastor isn't their beloved former pastor; within a year they step away to see how things will "shake out."

Slip Aways

These are people who were more or less "neutral" about pastoral change, but when the new pastor doesn't connect with them, for whatever reason, they simply slip away.

Fade Aways

They remain a year or two after the transition but fade away when the new pastor and changing church dynamics fail to live up to their expectations or preconceived notions.

Stow Aways

This group hangs around in the background without doing any work or contributing. They often exhibit either one of two specific behaviors: some often can be vocal at the most inopportune times, attempting to exercise sway over the direction of the church, usually from the stereotypical "we've never done it this way before" perspective. Others are quick to complain if they feel their personal needs and desires are not being met.

The incoming pastor should prepare to face all these dynamics and not be surprised by them. After all, this is the norm in any transition. The new pastor must *expect to work very hard to be a witness in word and by example to the Resurrected Christ!*

And Some New People Will Surface

Incoming pastors report with great joy the number of new people who come to the surface during the first hundred days. Whether these people take the form of people sitting on the sidelines or are new to the church community, it's an exhilarating experience for the newly arrived pastor. The categories below highlight the kinds of people who come to the surface:

Show Ups

Some new people will show up *because* there is pastoral change! Even where the previous pastor is held in high esteem, there are some people in the community who have formed a different opinion; maybe they ran into the pastor at the local Rotary club or soccer field and formed a negative opinion that has kept them from exploring the church. Now, with the change in pastors, they will check it out.

Step Ups

There are some spiritually mature people in a congregation who just intuitively know when the church needs a shot of adrenalin. They will somehow sense that some other people (and their giving) will step back.

So to the best of their ability, they will step up. They may be key leaders or folks barely known in the congregation. They may be charter members or relatively new. They may step up with extravagant generosity or sign on to volunteer in a needed ministry. But they will have one thing in common: their actions will surprise everyone!

Move Ups

These are the folks who had started moving into church leadership and now with the transition are called upon to "move up" sooner than they expected. And they will, bringing a whole new dimension to the church as it bridges from the past into the future. *(Be aware—sometimes "Move Ups" will threaten the existing structure and leaders.)*

Grow Ups

In every church there are people "young in their faith." They have already been involved in the discipleship process, and now during this time of transition, some will be growing up to take on more responsibility and leadership.

Ramp Ups

These are the dedicated "worker bees" who have been working hard, and the kind of people the church counts on. But the church had fallen into behaviors and patterns that unwittingly limited their own appraisal of what they could do. Now, with the transition new needs exist, and they find they "can do much more than they ever imagined." They ramp up their efforts and inspire a whole host of new people as well as the existing members.

Climb Ups

For reasons unknown, some folks will want to take advantage of the pastoral change to "climb up" the leadership ladder and seek to unduly influence—often for their own personal agenda.

Finally, and perhaps most importantly, expect the world and the church world at large to continue to change (macrochange), while a local congregation is going through a multitude of specific changes (microchange). Who knows what attendance patterns will be in the future? Who can really predict the impact of social media and alternative churches? Who can be prepared for how such forces as cultural changes, politics, stock market volatility, and increasing diversity are going to directly and indirectly impact the congregation…and the constantly changing church world which forms the backdrop of ministry? No one has all the answers.

Pastors can expect to be called on to reinvent themselves and their ministries multiple times over, expecting to minister to people who will be in varying stages of culture shock.

In his book, *Team of Teams: New Rules of Engagement for a Complex World*, retired Army General Stanley McChrystal observed—in referring to his leadership of the task force charged with fighting the decentralized, fast moving, always morphing Al Qaeda during the Iraqi War—that, "we had to develop a new paradigm of personal leadership. The role of the senior leader was no longer that of controlling puppet master, but rather that of an empathetic crafter of culture."[1] Incoming pastors should expect to face the ongoing rules of engagement by creating a culture that is adaptable, sustainable, and resilient

McChrystal makes the case that today's leadership is no longer about being a "chess master" with advanced tactical knowledge and brilliant strategy but being a "gardener" who brings teams of people together and empowers decision-making and action. This paradigm shift was difficult for him as a general, and for the entire military establishment. But, after repeated setbacks on the battlefield and within the war-torn county, the re-alization that the tried and true military strategy effectively used for genera-tions that had been based on top-down, command and control leadership was no longer working. (And it certainly won't work in the church.)

What is needed in leadership today—with all the fast-paced world's connectivity and interconnectedness through social media, are leaders (in-cluding pastors) who create a culture of teamwork that connects a wide ar-ray of people to a common purpose and mission. "The gardener," McChrys-tal observes, "cannot actually 'grow' tomatoes, squash, or beans—but can foster an environment in which the plants do so."[2]

General McChrystal has identified a leadership expectation for every incoming pastor: leaders must adapt their styles. Says the general, "Gar-deners plant and harvest, but more than anything, they *tend*. Plants are watered, beds are fertilized and weeds are removed. Long days are spent walking humid pathways or on sore knees examining fragile stalks. Regular visits by good gardeners are not pro forma gestures of concern—they leave the crop stronger. So it is with leaders."[3]

The incoming pastor calmly navigates the Changeover Zone, baton firmly in hand and expecting great things ahead.

What to Look for in a Second Pastor Following a Founder

No one ever drowned in sweat.

—Lou Holtz

W hat do you look for in a second pastor?" The question came in day one of a workshop for supervisors. Someone across the room shouted out immediately, "Not a savior, that's for sure!" After the laughter subsided, the man who asked the question continued. "The reason I'm here is that we've had bad experiences with every one of our new church plants that has changed pastors. Two of four closed within just a few months after the change. Two others appear to be on life support." As he spoke, the woman who had shouted her reply nodded in agreement.

Sadly, this is an oft-repeated story describing what happens when founding pastors depart their church and the second pastor in a church's young history arrives. And we often say in our workshops for potential second pastors: "You arrive as their minister; you have to earn the right to be their pastor. And this will take time."

In the preceding pages we outlined some specific ways to move the dynamic from "minister" to "pastor" in as short a time as feasible, all the while creating a good, healthy culture when the incoming pastor arrives to the new church.

To help us understand better what improves the chances for a good transition and to help us identify and train good candidates, we commissioned the Lewis Center to do a study of second pastors, that is, those pastors who followed directly behind the founding pastor of a church. Their research team surveyed second pastors who had successfully followed a founder and led with the kind of effectiveness and fruitfulness necessary

88

to grow a vibrant, healthy congregation. (See appendix for the complete study.)

From their work, we gleaned some valuable insights. The following Essential Seven Characteristics capture the advice that these pastors would give to candidates who are looking to become second pastors:

1. Positive attitude

2. Patience

3. Self-confidence

4. Good listener

5. Thick skin

6. Vision

7. Flexibility

These characteristics are essential because when a new church is going through its first pastoral transition, four parties—the supervisor, the exiting pastor, the arriving pastor, and the local church—tend to greatly underestimate the emotional complexities and trauma experienced by the receiving church. The core character of the new pastor will be tested quickly.

Add to these the "8 Great Skills" we distilled from the study. These skills are what effective second pastors tell us are needed to be successful:

1. Relational intentionality

2. The ability to learn existing church culture and respond appropriately to it

3. A passionate communicator

4. The ability to develop and apply systems

5. The willingness and ability to raise money

6. Effectiveness in vision casting

7. The ability to identify and respond to needs of mission field

8. Adept at change management with patience

Of course, most of the characteristics and skills apply to any pastor in any situation! But there are a few nonnegotiables that the study and our experience bears witness to:

- Does your candidate have an affinity for and match the community?

- Does the candidate match the DNA of the new church?

- Does the candidate have a "whatever it takes" work ethic?

- Does the candidate embrace systems to achieve goals?

- Is the candidate eagerly expecting to stay at least six to twelve years?

- Does the candidate have a proven track record of moving a single-cell organization to multiple cells?

A last word about affinity when potential second pastors are being considered: selections that go against affinity match and/or DNA match place all parties at great risk of failure. Reasoning such as "we can train them to overcome these obstacles" ignores the realities.

Competencies and skills effective in one church don't necessarily transfer to another one. Affinities that help the pastor to connect in one church don't necessarily make the same connections in another. A significant number of young churches trace difficult struggles to the lack of an "affinity match" between the incoming pastor and the community served by the church.

COACHING TIP: Are there exceptions? Very rarely, but when there are this is what we see: the new pastor has a track record bearing fruit in cross-cultural settings.

Young churches are most vulnerable when they face the loss of their founder and pass through their first pastoral transition. Churches often do not survive the first pastoral transition for a multitude of reasons, and none of which might be at all related to the new pastor.

However, when the incoming pastor disproportionately displays any of the following seven deadly sins it will guarantee difficult days ahead for the church:

1. Minimal spiritual passion or depth

2. Little awareness of healthy personal and relational boundaries

3. Little discussion or interest in growing church numerically

4. Lack of personal and professional maturity

5. Poor work ethic

6. Critical spirit reflecting a "know it all" attitude

7. Driven by personal agenda: more "me" than "we"

COACHING TIP: Don't be fooled by characteristics and skills that surface during an assessment interview. A candidate's actual track record can be more important than his or her skills!

Many supervisors have been honest enough to share the most common mistakes they make when identifying and deploying second pastors or pastors following a long-tenured pastorate:

1. Not vetting the preaching skills

2. Not utilizing any recognized assessment tools (such as the DISC profile, Strength Finders, etc.)

3. Minimizing the need for a proven "track record"

4. Overlooking public leadership roles and how the candidate handles them

5. Undervaluing "relational intentionality" and affinity

6. Not staying in the Changeover Zone long enough with the incoming pastor to manage a smooth transition

We are frequently asked by judicatories to do three things: (1) help assess potential candidates for following a founder or a long-tenured pastor, (2) help create a pool of trained candidates, and (3) help establish protocols and practices for the supervisors to utilize when it comes to making decisions about following a founder or long-tenured pastor. More and more we are also asked by local congregations to help them to say "goodbye" and "hello" at the same time, and to accelerate their church's growth during a time of pastoral transition.

Pastoral transitions have so many moving parts that it is easy for someone to "drop the baton" and for mistakes to be made. But grace abounds! Most—but not all—mistakes can be overcome with intentionality, good coaching, utilizing proven practices, and a congregational commitment to the ministry of the church.... And lots of prayer!

FOLLOWING THE LONG-TENURED PASTOR

The church is filled with skeptics, often about the church in general. Even good-hearted folk who have stayed through a lot of church wars have built up big doses of skepticism of "the system" that is going to send them their new pastor, or by which they are going to "call" their new pastor.

This can be especially true in a church that has been pastored by a long-tenured leader. If the church has been successful reaching its mission field, then it has probably grown by adding many from outside its denomination, many of whom will have only ever experienced the current pastor. They have formed close ties and deep bonds. Others, who have been there a long time, will draw upon muscle memory to remind themselves (and their friends) that "we've gone through this before."

But their skepticism is often tempered by their adoration of the long-tenured pastor. Folks overlook flaws and even what they consider to be their own personal disagreements with the pastor whom they have long known and loved. In either case, it may prove difficult for many folks to deal with the reality of getting a new pastor. Questions will abound!

Differences and Similarities

Founding Pastors and Long-Tenured Pastors

Real champions do not become champions when they win the event,
but in the hours, weeks, months and years they spend preparing for it.
—T. Alan Armstrong

Any pastoral transition involving either a founder or a long-tenured pastor requires the same level of scrutiny and attention. The following observations will help stimulate the thought processes of supervisors and church leaders about how to improve pastoral transitions in their respective churches. (See appendix.)

Similarities

There are many often-observed similarities between *successful* new church start situations and *successful* long-tenured pastorate situations:

1. Both enjoy long tenure. The new church start going through its first pastoral transition is usually seven to ten years old; for a long-tenured pastorate going through a pastoral change, it's about double that number and sometimes longer. (Compared to the average pastoral tenure nationally for all denominations and independents, which is 3.6 years according to Lifeway Research.)

2. Both the founding pastor and the long-tenured pastor:
   - are effective vision casters;
   - are considered by their respective congregations to be a friend;

- have earned admiration and credibility;
- will have a base of fierce loyalty, even amidst critics;
- have relationally intertwined roots with many, based on significant "marker moments" of pastoral involvement in congregants' lives.

3. Upon their departure, the founding pastor and the long-tenured pastor both:
    - feel deeply invested in the church's success now and for the future;
    - will see angst and hurt among many when they leave the congregation;
    - play a critical role in "passing the baton" to their successor;
    - are instrumental in helping the church they love deal with the stages of grief at their leaving.

Differences

"Good pastorates" come in all shapes and sizes. Assuming a "good pastorate," we have compiled, from workshops and churches and pastors with whom we have worked, this list of perceived differences between a successful (a) new church start situation; (b) long-tenured pastorate (ten or more years), and (c) shorter-term pastor (two to five years).

1. Relationship of pastor to congregation
    - New Church Planter (NCP) "births a baby."
    - Long-Tenured Pastorate (LTP) "adopts a child" and builds relationships over time.
    - Shorter-Term Pastor (STP) "fosters children" with great love but often not as deeply developed a sense of permanency or ownership.

2. Relationships of pastor within congregation
    - NCP is often the relational hub for the congregation.
    - LTP has become the relational architect, designing systems to promote relationships.

- STP is relationally invested but not the center or architect of relationships within the congregation.

3. Observable dynamics of pastor with congregation
   - NCP church "centers around pastor"; the younger the church, the more observable.
   - LTP "coalesces around pastor"; the longer the tenure, the more observable.
   - STP congregation "connects with pastor"; the more relational the pastor, the more observable.

4. Culture creation
   - NCP created culture from start.
   - LTP crystalizes culture over time and positively contextualizes it to her or his tenure.
   - STP connects to existing culture but has little time or credibility to intentionally change or improve it.

5. Values formation
   - NCP instills and protects values from the start.
   - LTP inspires and strengthens values and over time facilitates values clarification.
   - STP identifies with and communicates existing values.

6. Spiritual dynamics
   - NCP is seen as a spiritual parent (guide, guru, and so on).
   - LTP is seen as a spiritual mentor (giant, guru, and so on).
   - STP is seen as a spiritual champion (cheerleader, fellow-searcher, and so on).

7. Tribal or corporate knowledge awareness.
   - In NCP, polity and procedures are not well known or appreciated—younger, more observable.
   - In LTP, there is high knowledge and appreciation in leaders—less awareness among newer members.
   - In STP, there is high corporate knowledge because of multiple transitions—often high skepticism.

8. Pastoral relationships
   - NCP: Only pastor ever known by some; only pastor at this church by all; deep roots.

- LTP: Only pastor known by many if not most newer at-tenders; deep roots.
- STP: Known and loved multiple pastors; roots not as deep.

If demographers are right that an aging clergy population is fast approaching retirement, leaving many churches to experience the departure of long-tenured pastors, then how these transitions are handled will have a great impact on the future ministry of their respective churches. Better to take a page from those organizations that do "succession" planning than be surprised at the last minute. More and more churches have witnessed the need for Changeover Zone training. By inviting all their pastors within this retirement horizon, church networks and denominations help reduce anxiety and fear on the part of clergy and churches.

Churches that are being led by a long-tenured pastor benefit greatly from at least beginning the conversations about transition when the Changeover Zone is still on the horizon, even up to a few years away. Again, good conversations done from a healthy perspective and for strategic planning reduce worry and anxiety on the part of the congregation and the soon-retiring pastor. The earlier transition conversations begin—especially if the pastor's retirement is in the equation—the better.

To facilitate a smooth and seamless passing of the baton more and more churches are working proactively with both supervisors and local leaders to bring in the successor—up to a year or two in advance of the current pastor's retirement. This front-end approach easily affords churches the luxury to pass the baton in a longer Changeover Zone.

Chapter 15

Planning a Succession or a "Planned Succession"?

Even if you are on the right track you get run over if you just sit there.

—Will Rogers

C arl is not retiring for two years, but we want to be sure we get this right!" Cheryl's voice was strong and determined as she spoke to her church's personnel committee. Their beloved pastor of twenty years would be departing, and the church would receive a new pastor, which was already creating some anxiety in the congregation. She added, "It will require a lot of advance preparation!"

Not only was Cheryl a dedicated member of the church, but her career in the corporate world, as well as having worked many years for a national not-for-profit, made her ideal to lead the church's effort to steer the pastoral transition. To prepare her church to enter the Changeover Zone, she contracted with a consultant who specialized in pastoral transitions... *two years in advance*! Her corporate experience had taught her that advance planning significantly improves the odds of a healthy transition in any organization, including her church. The more advance warning that a long-tenured pastor is leaving, the more the odds increase to have a healthy transition. More and more churches and judicatories—both anticipating and reeling from the rising tide of retirements—are using third-party consultants to assist in "planning succession."

Creg Lutz is a member of the University of Texas relay team. Because of his determined attitude, he grew from a scrawny kid into a star athlete, highly recruited by the top universities in the country. Listen to him describe how he prepares before he even steps on the track. "But long before that [the race] I 'prepare to prepare' by countless hours of conditioning, committing to the right kind of diet, by getting mentally tough, by getting my attitude sharp so that my body, mind, and spirit are right...long before I step on the track and charge into the changeover zone."

This kind of preparation is commonly known in organizational circles as a "planned succession." In planned successions, there are a number of key steps taken *before and in preparation for* entering the Changeover Zone. Consequently, wise planning increases the length of time to carry out the transition, on the front end.

Such succession planning transitions are the rule for churches and/or denominations that practice a "call" approach to the deployment of clergy. Planned successions are, however, the rare exception—but becoming more common—in denominations that practice a "sent" approach to deploying clergy, where pastors are "appointed" or "assigned" by their supervisors to their respective churches.

Ending Well: Two Stories

Consider the stories of two pastors' journeys: Jason and Elizabeth, both seminary students who pursued pastoral ministry.

Jason, a highly respected, non denominational pastor, met Elizabeth, a United Methodist pastor, while in seminary. Jason had entered seminary from the United Methodist church in which he had grown up, but for reasons theological and personal, had opted to fulfill his ministry in another setting.

Now, Jason was tired. He had worked hard for a very long time. He was proud of what God had accomplished through his hard work. But now he was more tired than anything. It wasn't the work that had worn him out; it was the fear. And now, he must face that fear, like it or not. Even while tired, Jason remembered what had driven him so hard in ministry back when he was a young pastor just getting started: the passion to make a kingdom difference and the determination to right some of the wrongs he perceived in the church at large—to participate in its revival.

And so his ministry began. During college a youth ministry job opened up, and then expanded. He attended a noted seminary and was hired on as an associate minister in a local congregation. After graduation, he took another associate position. A few years later, Jason answered the call to become the minister of another church. But the ache in his heart for reviving the church did not diminish.

He had heard from colleagues and in conferences about the advantages of starting a new church: Cast your own vision! No pre-existing problems! Set your own DNA and culture! Expand the kingdom witness! All these appealed to his sense of "fixing the church." And so began a twenty-five-year journey: starting from nothing and building a community of faith around the basics of Christian discipleship. And his dream turned into reality. Many people joined and found themselves transformed along the many years of encountering and following Christ.

Jason, fulfilled by the unfolding of his dream, found himself satisfied and challenged at the same time. The work of ministry had proved hard, of that he had no illusions. But the hardships seemed miniscule compared to the transformed lives he witnessed. However, he now faced the greatest challenge of his ministry and life: he needed to retire. Not due to lack of passion but rather lack of energy. He found himself less patient with others, more tired from doing routines that used to thrill him, and he recognized the need for much younger leadership.

What scared him was not only the ending of his ministry but also worries about who would take over "his baby," the church he had started so many years ago. Of course, he knew the church belonged to God, but Jason had raised her, nurtured her, grown her, and led her; and now he faced the task of leaving her. "Am I abandoning her?" he often asked himself during sleepless nights. For months, he awakened with the dread of, "How do I leave well?"

He broached the subject with his wife, Karen, who had no trouble in telling him it was time to leave. She had seen his spirit waning the last few years, and much as she loved the church and the many relationships she had developed, she knew it was time for them to sever ties. Perhaps, she reasoned, after a year or so of being away, they could return as "just members" of their church.

Jason then approached the lay leader of the church, who initially tried to talk him out of it. It was hard for him to comprehend that the pastor who had married him and his wife, who had officiated at his father's funeral, who had baptized all three of his children, could actually want to quit when he still seemed so effective. After a few meetings, however, he too recognized the wisdom of Jason's decision. A series of meetings with the leadership council allowed the leaders to digest Jason's decisions and consider the consequences and rollout of his departure.

As the lay leader informed other leaders, the church's leadership were a bit surprised (some say stunned) with the realization that immediately after their grief had set in, fear and dread (some say anger) quickly followed. Now it was their turn to experience the same thought that had gripped Jason: What did the future hold for their church? Most had experienced only him as their pastor, and no one else. Now they faced the task of managing the change throughout the congregation and finding their beloved pastor's replacement. How does a church find a replacement for the only pastor it has ever known? What competencies should they look for? How should they announce this to the church? Are there proper protocols for this?

During a meeting where these questions occupied the agenda, one of the church council members noted that her business and many others had developed a succession plan, whereby certain executives followed an exit plan as they approached retirement. While this seemed helpful, many dismissed the idea with the thought, "Well, that's business. We are running a church here, and that doesn't apply to us. Through prayer and the Holy Spirit, God will show us the way, and we can figure out the details."

And so for months, Jason and his council met and wondered and discussed and wondered and went around in circles, until someone said, "I see no reason to even tell the congregation yet; let's just hire an associate and see if that person works out and can be groomed to be Jason's successor. Then when we do let everyone know Jason is retiring, we'll have his successor in place and all will be well." The council, now fatigued and frustrated from countless meetings and endless discussions, agreed this seemed the prudent course of action.

And so it was decided. The council, fortified by each other, voted to keep Jason's retirement quiet until an associate/"closet replacement" was hired, and Jason would have the freedom to personally recruit his successor from his wide sphere of friendships, national church associations, and influence. Everyone began to sleep much better.

Except Jason. Late at night, questions continued to exist: How do we know this is the proper way to leave? Are we keeping information from the church? Won't they chafe at not knowing? What if the associate—even if he is a good friend—is not the right person? What if after we start working together we discover that we don't actually agree on the vision forward? What then? In many ways at this scary time, Jason wished somebody else could make these tough decisions and be accountable for them; in some ways he even yearned for his old Methodist roots and its system for changing pastors.

Elizabeth, his old friend from seminary days, faced the same fears as Jason. They had actually been in regular e-mail contact about their respective decisions to retire. She also had worked hard over a storied ministry career; for her it was a second career and her ministry had benefitted from her previous training and work experience in marketing in the corporate world. Following a short span as an associate pastor right out of seminary, she had been appointed by the bishop as the pastor of a struggling urban church. She stabilized it and slowed its numerical decline, and after just a few years was appointed as district superintendent to serve on the bishop's cabinet and supervise some seventy other local churches in the area. Five years into that assignment, she was appointed to be the second pastor who followed the founding pastor of the fast-growing new church Point of Light UMC. She distinguished herself once more, but it was a tough ten-year tenure of again stabilizing and accelerating a church's growth.

She, like Jason, was tired, and for many of the same reasons. Point of Light had grown into being a unique church, quite noticeable in the United Methodist world for its emphasis on creativity, vibrant small group ministry, contemporary worship, and missional DNA. Because of this, and because Elizabeth herself had once served on the bishop's cabinet that deploys pastors to the denomination's churches, she took it upon herself to bring together her district superintendent and bishop so she could ask if the three of them could consider some alternative methods to sending Point of Light its next pastor. She was worried that the traditional way of "appointing" its next pastor (a system she generally wholeheartedly supported) would not be the best approach, following her long-tenured pastorate.

She suggested that Point of Light be allowed to develop a planned succession—in which she and the church would have a more significant voice than usual—to identify and embed her successor in the congregation by being appointed to the church *a year in advance* and work with Elizabeth in her final year before retirement. This would, Elizabeth argued, allow the incoming pastor to learn the unique culture and DNA of Point of Light, as well as allow Elizabeth to "pass the baton" over a longer period of time so that by the time she retired, her successor would already be "off to a running start."

Even as she made the request, Elizabeth had her fears. She feared her colleagues would be critical of her stretching the "system" in ways it wasn't used to; she feared what might happen in the year overlap if the two pastors didn't get along, or if it appeared they weren't on the same page; she feared it wouldn't work. She and Jason had discussed the differences in how pastoral transitions were made in their respective systems; and right now, fearing for who would become the pastor to take over her beloved church, she wished she could do it more like Jason.

Jason's story is not a new one. We have consulted with dozens and dozens of pastors and church leaders facing similar questions. Elizabeth's story is a little newer within mainline denominations, and we likewise have consulted with dozens and dozens of pastors, bishops, cabinets, and churches going through similar transitions.

Is there a proper protocol for leaving a church, and leaving it well? Of course there is. Many characters in the Bible handed over the leadership baton to a younger leader; you read about many of them in chapter 2. In the next few pages we'll share some thoughts gleaned from our experiences with churches exploring a planned succession and what we teach in our workshops regarding preparing to leave. It comes from many interactions and extensive field experience. For some groups it may seem beyond their normal practices for pastoral transitions, but remember that not all transitions are equal; exceptions apply.

Fortunately, Jason contacted us and we consulted with his leaders about what constitutes a healthy succession. He recommended Elizabeth connect with us and we worked with her, the bishop and cabinet, and the church to develop a good transition journey. Even though they came from different tribal protocols, both journeys followed the textbook, and they ended well. Jason and his wife stayed in the area, enjoyed retirement, and after twelve months returned to their church and joined it. They love their new pastor and flourish under her leadership. Elizabeth and her husband moved to another state to be near children, and left the church in a healthy, vibrant, growing mode because her successor entered in and charged out of the Changeover Zone with confidence and credibility.

Here is a rough outline we coached both Jason and Elizabeth to use. Keep in mind denominational protocols and tribal settings and the need to tweak any approach to the context and setting. But from Episcopalian to Pentecostal to nondenominational, we have seen this work well when it comes to planned successions:

1. An extended, healthy timeline (from decision to leave until new pastor arrives) tends to be approximately eighteen months. Remember, there is "preparation" even to get ready to enter the Changeover Zone.

2. Hire a third party to consult with and walk through the necessary conversations. Lean heavily on the consultant, who can remain emotionally detached enough to ask the right questions and keep the process moving along.

3. If the pastor is married, please include the spouse in all matters of discernment and decision-making. Ignoring this diminishes the special role they have played in the church.

4. If applicable, inform and engage the denominational supervisor. Often, denominational supervisors insist on managing all aspects of the timing, announcements, and execution.

5. Inform the chair of the church personnel committee.

6. Inform the official leaders of the church.

7. Have the departing pastor and spouse make a list of special friends in the church to inform of their leaving in private conversations. Confidentiality is paramount. (Do not meet with groups, but rather, couples or individuals.)

8. When the timing is right and after decisions have been made that the pastor will be leaving (and when), the board writes a letter (posted on a Monday) to the church informing them of the pastor's departure, with a general timeline outlined.

COACHING TIP: As a matter of course, upsetting or anxiety-provoking news should be digested first in private; never in a public gathering.

9. For approximately two weeks, the pastor and spouse and church leaders should not receive or respond to phone calls, e-mails, social media, and so forth inquiring about the departure. In our experience, the vast majority of these inquiries are looking for something hidden and wrong things are said. Failure to heed this warning has torpedoed many a succession plan.

10. A week after the letter goes out, a church spokesperson (not the pastor) reads the letter during Sunday morning worship with an additional note that says, "As we gain better clarity, we will keep you informed immediately." And, "These are exciting times; we understand you may have some anxieties, but let's keep the future in prayer, as well as our pastor during this time of transition."

11. Discussion now centers on the successor: Identify competencies and affinities needed. (Warning: The tendency is to attempt to overcorrect and/or find someone who can serve primarily the existing members.) Succession seems to work best when leaders/supervisors find a much younger and less experienced minister.

12. Avoid letting the departing pastor choose his or her

replacement. While certainly input is invited, the departing minister often cannot emotionally detach enough to make good decisions and think clearly. Plus, they often fall to the temptation to have their successor "maintain" what they have accomplished, which may not accelerate the church's growth into the future.

13. Since many transitions happen in unique circumstances, give strong consideration to the use of an intentional interim, even if the new pastor has already been identified.

14. Often it can be helpful to time the transition so that the departing pastor leaves the church in the winter quarter (January-March), leaving time for the incoming pastor to lead the church through Holy Week.

15. Follow the best practices outlined in chapter 4 about saying goodbye to the departing pastor. At minimum, hold a public gathering to celebrate the ministry of the departing pastor at least two weeks before he or she preaches for the last time.

16. The departing pastor must respect professional boundaries by ceasing conversation with members of the church, with few exceptions. If they remain in the area, we suggest a twelve-month leave of absence and then decide if it is possible to return.

These steps begin (but are not always completed) before the church actually enters the Changeover Zone, as we have described it in the book. Even though your church might not be able to—or choose to—follow each one of these "Preparing to Prepare" steps, we hope you will aim to accomplish as many as possible in your setting. The steps are intended as guidelines for the tone and protocol that can lead to either a healthy succession planning or even an official planned succession. Remember, a church usually enters the Changeover Zone about one hundred days before the pastoral change actually occurs; but in a planned succession, as well as in most successful succession planning situations involving a long-tenured or retiring pastor, you can begin planning to enter the Changeover Zone up to a year or more in advance.

Inheriting the Church They've Always Wanted

Running is a perfect metaphor for life because you get out of it what you put into it.

—Oprah Winfrey

Martha died on September 1, 1914, a little before 1:00 p.m. Her death is now a historic moment and—at least among environmentalists and scientists—was nationally celebrated on its one hundredth anniversary. Martha indeed was special. Her death marks perhaps the only time scientists have been able to pinpoint the exact date and time that a species became extinct. Martha was the most famous passenger pigeon of all time. Just a few decades earlier—as they had done for centuries—passenger pigeons filled the skies in the millions. She was the last of a kind, and at her death, the entire species was gone.[1]

We mention this only because some have suggested, and written rather poetically, that the "Christian church is just one generation from being extinct."[2] We don't actually buy into that theological sentiment totally, but we do get the idea behind it: Is the Christian baton being picked up by the succeeding generation? While we don't mean to be overly dramatic, it does seem true that how adept we become at passing the baton of the faith from one generation to the other makes all the difference to the future.

Perhaps if we become more effective at passing the baton from leader to leader, we'll become better at passing the baton from follower to follower.

"U.S. hits rock bottom with dropped batons!" shouted out sports columnist of the Associated Press. The men's and women's Olympic teams had both suffered embarrassing defeats in the 2008 Olympics in China, even with arguably superior athletes. Why? Because outstanding athletes hadn't learned to work well enough as a team to successfully pass the baton from one superstar to another!

In so many ventures in life striving for long-term viability and growth, it is the quality of the leadership hand-off from the current leader to successor that makes the difference between success and failure. So it is with the church when it comes to what happens in the Changeover Zone. In short, we can't afford to be sloppy if we want to ensure that the church won't become extinct.

Denominations and related church groups invest millions of dollars to train new pastors, provide first-class seminaries, and undergird churches with all sorts of financial support. Christ's church claims a glorious history and a sacred mandate; yet among many there is the feeling that "the church" (especially the mainline church) continues to struggle and lose influence in its respective mission fields.

We frequently hear from supervisors that the lack of young talent, that "our shallow bench strength," is one of the primary reasons for the relentless, unsettling decline within mainline Christianity. Some of that feeling, no doubt, may stem from the quality (or lack of quality) of talent we have taking hold of the reigns of leadership, but much of it is the quality of the handoff that happens in the Changeover Zone. Our work with pastoral transitions has led us to wonder if the problem isn't that "we lack the talent," but that we have dropped the baton when it comes to leadership passing the baton in the Changeover Zone. How many members, how many attenders, how much community respect do we lose when we drop the baton during a pastoral transition? We sure hear such painful, heart-wrenching stories virtually everywhere we work.

But does it have to be that way? No! We hope that this book has helped cast a vision within churches and judicatories and among pastors that what happens in the Changeover Zone can create a culture of success and fruitfulness, even during a pastoral transition and long into the future.

Why? Because—as a participant in a workshop once moaned—when a church receives a new pastor, that pastor is "inheriting the church *they've* always wanted!" It's true. The church the new pastor is going to has hopes and dreams, strengths and weaknesses, challenges and opportunities, problems and its possibilities. The leaders and members hold dear to some dream (or fantasy) of what their church is and what they want it to be. Most folks love their church and can't wait for their new pastor to love it as well. Most want their church to be as impactful for new people as it has been for them. Still, some folks will have their personal agenda and expect the new pastor to meet it; other folks will have cherished anchors in the past and be fearful of the future under a new leader.

It is a daunting task for that new pastor to learn the congregation and earn the people's trust; to share in their culture and help shape it anew; to discern the needs of the community and direct the pace at which the church can meet them; to love the sheep deeply and stretch them appropriately; to transition from "yesterday" to "today" to "tomorrow" in a healthy way; to go from being "the new minister" to truly becoming "their pastor." If a baton is dropped needlessly and these things do not happen, everyone suffers and God weeps.

Most of the time the newly arriving pastor is competent, eager, ready, and excited to be there. The new pastor grasps and affirms what the congregation thinks their church is in reality. But sometimes, the pastor must help the church look clearer at itself, at its potential, and at its promise if it is to be the church God wants it to be. When good things happen in the Changeover Zone, these needed conversations are possible because of trust and respect.

And sometimes the new pastor brings her or his own dreams (fantasy) of what the church is and what he or she wants it to become. Other times, unknowingly and inappropriately the new pastor tries to make their new church into the church she or he has always wanted. There are times when the pastor is ill equipped and not well trained and charges in with a domineering attitude and without needed sensitivity. If these things happen, and a baton is dropped needlessly, everyone suffers and God weeps.

What happens in the Changeover Zone hopefully brings out the best in the church, the arriving pastor, the exiting pastor, and the supervisors. When that happens, "the church they've always wanted" soon refers to the congregation *and* the pastor. And all the players—supervisors, church, exiting pastor, arriving pastor—can be part of making it a church God has always wanted!

Mission-Field Matrix

We have already discussed why a church going through its first pastoral transition is at risk. Let's take some time now for you—as a developer or district superintendent (DS)—to assess the context and risk of the specific new church or churches in your Conference?

Using this "Mission Field Matrix" write a short paragraph that describes your "gut-level" feel regarding the open church receiving its first new pastor:

1. The church

2. The community

3. Potential successors

4. Tribal connections

Here are four critical considerations that should be included in your narrative:

1. The church: Is it strong? Chartered? Age? Average Worship Attendance? Relationship w/mother church? Growth trends? Weekly giving? Over-all Financial condition? Meeting place? Lay leadership? Pastoral leadership? Culture? DNA? Worship style? Maturity? Specific concerns? Conflict? Weaknesses?

2. The community: population makeup and growth trends: ethnicity, age levels, education, socio-economic factors, religious involvement? Relationship with other churches? How is church meeting felt needs of the community? How involved is founder in the community?

3. Potential successors: How deep is talent pool? Is there someone who seems ideal or promising as a successor? Are potential successors trained as second pastors? Does the conference have ability to provide coaching, mentoring, training?

4. Tribal Connections: What is relationship with mother church? How connected does church appear to be with denomination? Have DS and Developer been trained in Following the Founder?

Transition Template

The Church	The Community

Bench Strength	Tribal Connections

Considering these critical questions write a brief gut-level narrative assessing where the church is going in the transition:

1. **The Church:**
   Is it strong? Chartered? Age? Average Worship Attendance? Relationship w/mother church? Growth trends? Weekly giving? Over-all financial condition? Meeting

place? Lay leadership? Pastoral leadership? Culture? DNA? Worship style? Maturity? Specific concerns? Conflict? Weaknesses?

2. **The Community:**
   Population makeup and growth trends: ethnicity, age levels, education, socio-economic factors, religious involvement? Relationship with other churches? Is church meeting felt needs of the community? Is founder involved in the community?

3. **Bench Strength:**
   How deep is talent pool? Are there potential successors who seem ideal or promising? Are potential successors trained as second pastors? Does the conference have ability to provide coaching, mentoring, and training?

4. **Tribal Connections:**
   What is relationship with mother church? How connected does church appear to be with denomination? Have DS and Developer been trained in Following the Founder?

Transition Template Continuum

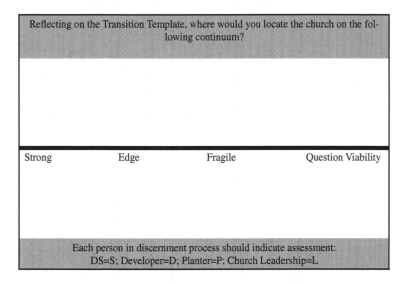

Reflecting on the Transition Template, where would you locate the church on the following continuum?

Strong	Edge	Fragile	Question Viability

Each person in discernment process should indicate assessment:
DS=S; Developer=D; Planter=P; Church Leadership=L

Note: A church assessed to be on the right of Transition Template continuum doesn't mean you can't or shouldn't make the move, but it is an indicator of how much intentional support the conference/district will need to provide: coaching, appropriate leadership training seminars & workshops, mentoring, time involvement on the part of the DS and developer. In certain situation it could also possibly mean extending the project funding for additional months.

Second Pastor Assessment Guide

While there is no scientific way to find the right person, at the right time, in the right mission field, we have assessment conversations using the following language (*this should be grace-filled, not pharisaic*).

Ideal

Great affinity match, excellent skills, winning personality, proven track record in similar context, unquestioned commitment to denomination, passionate about the gospel, likely to "connect" immediately. Virtually everyone in appointment discernment would say, "He/she would be perfect!"

Promising

Adequate affinity match, developing skill set, positive personality, proven track record, unquestioned commitment to denomination, passionate about the gospel, ability to "connect" over time. Most in discernment process would say, "I think she/he would be great there!"

Acceptable

Winning personality but perhaps not immediate affinity with the specific mission field in question; OR candidate is best of shallow talent pool but has possibility to grow in the assignment. Good skill set and preaching style, relational awareness, unquestioned commitment to denomination, yet there are noticeable questions or hesitancy not only on the part of the candidate but on those in supervisory capacities. Most in discernment process would say, "I can see that working." (Be careful about "talking ourselves into it.")

Risky

Low affinity match, developing skill set, lack of track record, unquestioned commitment to denomination but supervisors may question abilities and/or leadership; passionate about the gospel but uncertain about "connecting" or communicating with the kind of professionalism we expect out of clergy. Most in discernment process would say something like, "I just don't see it." This is a good time to consider an intentional interim. (Caution! Are we "talking ourselves into it"?)

Avoid (If Possible)

Mismatched affinity, questionable track record, mediocre skill set, negative attitude, low self-awareness. Usually these candidates appear because there is an extremely shallow bench. Those in discernment process say something like, "We've got to send somebody there." This is a good time for an intentional interim (or to hold off making an appointment change if you can).

REMEMBER: A candidate should be assessed FOR a specific church and mission field, not just that she/he would be a good second pastor in general. A mismatched affinity runs the risk of neutralizing an otherwise good skill set. Great affinity often allows time for skills to develop.

Sample Recruitment Letter

Colleagues,

Please check out this invitation to be part of a specialized training event for just a handful of clergy in the conference; we are also inviting DS's who may be available and intent on improving pastoral transitions.

"Following the Founder: Becoming a Successful Second Pastor"

Date/time/location

Throughout United Methodism, hundreds of new churches in a variety of settings are being planted or have recently been planted. It is becoming increasing clear that we need to have a trained pool of potential "second pastors" who will one day follow the planter.

Why this training?

Because no matter the age or condition of a church, when it has its first pastoral change...it is at risk. Hundreds of thousands of dollars have been invested; participants have given their heart and time as well as money to grow a church...and it can all be lost when the founder leaves, *if* the transition is not well thought out and implemented.

That is why I am contacting you: We are putting together a pool of trained "second pastors" to be ready when a new church has its first pastoral transition, and you have been suggested as a potential candidate.

Why you?

- A recent study by the Lewis Center for Church Leadership identified the following "6 Essential Characteristics": (1) patience, (2) self-confidence, (3) good listener, (4) thick skin, (5) vision, (6) flexibility

- In addition, the study identified "The 8 great skills needed": (1) ability to learn existing church culture and respond appropriately to it, (2) passionate communicator, (3) ability to develop & apply systems, (4) personal & professional maturity, (5) vision casting, (6) ability to identify & respond to needs of mission field, (7) clarity of Call to Ministry; (8) change agent with patience.

Does this description fit you?

This training for DS's, church developers, and potential second pastors is designed to help you discern if this might be a ministry area for you sometime in the future. The following individuals are receiving this invitation—would you have other friends to suggest? Thanks. *[list those invited]*

Please understand that completing this training should not imply that you would in fact be appointed as second pastor, or that we necessarily have immediate openings—only that you may be included in our pool of trained pastors to possibly follow a founder.

[Registration info]

[signature]

Successful Second Pastors: Excerpt from Lewis Center Study

Second Pastor Study
Findings about Pastors Who Follow Founding Pastors

A Research Project Commissioned by the North Texas
Conference, United Methodist Church
Lewis Center for Church Leadership, Wesley Theological
Seminary, Washington, DC
Lovett H. Weems, Jr., Project Director
Joe Arnold, Research Manager
Donald R. House, Consultant

Some Highlights from the Study

- Second pastors are not typically transitional pastors; they stay as long on average as founding pastors.

- Second pastors overwhelmingly describe their relationship with the founding pastor as good.

- There are not wholesale staff changes when the second pastor arrives. Over 75 percent of clergy and lay staff are still in place one year later.

- Second pastors give most of their time in the first year to worship and sermon preparation, leadership development, getting to know people, and evangelism.

- A majority of the churches receiving a second pastor experienced significant conflict in the year before the pastoral change.

- Second pastors see themselves as different from their predecessors in personality and approach to ministry, but attendance is greater if the two pastors are more similar.

- Second pastors report a strong match between their personal characteristics and the culture of their new congregations, and attendance is greater if the second pastor better matches the church's DNA.

- They report being similar to the predominant population the church is seeking to reach in terms of age, race, education, family, and background.

- Second pastors need patience, self-confidence, listening skills, thick skin, and flexibility.

- Pastors become second pastors around age 40 on average. Attendance is greater the older the second pastor is upon arrival—up to age 42. This indicates the ideal age of a second pastor is somewhat older than the ideal age of new church planters, where growth is more associated with very young clergy.

- Attendance grows with time during the tenure of the second pastor but at a decreasing rate, a common pattern for this phase of a new church no matter who is pastor.

Report Summary

Background

While many studies report on the work of church planters, few studies exist on the experience of second pastors—those who follow founding pastors of new congregations. The North Texas Conference of the United Methodist Church, hoping to address the vacuum, commissioned the Lewis Center for Church Leadership to study United Methodist second pastors from recent decades.

Conference congregational development staff persons identified just over 100 second pastors. Of this number, 56 completed an extensive survey.

This information and statistical analysis of various factors and their connections, if any, with attendance change during the second pastor's tenure provide the basis for the findings reported. Don House, PhD, of RRC, Inc., was engaged to do the regression analysis.

The 56 survey respondents serve in 15 different annual conferences: Central Texas, Dakotas, Florida, Greater New Jersey, Kansas East, Louisiana, Mississippi, North Alabama, North Carolina, North Georgia, North Texas, Southwest Texas, Texas, Virginia, and Western North Carolina

What We Learned

In terms of gender and age, **second pastors on average tend to be men around age 40**, although about 10 percent of those surveyed are women and the age range extends from 28 to 58.

By and large **second pastors are not interim or transitional pastors.** The founding pastors they follow had served on average 7 years. Second pastors who have already moved to another appointment stayed on average 6 years with about 10 percent staying 10 or more years. Almost 50 percent of second pastors responding to the survey have not yet moved since becoming a second pastor.

About **60 percent of the churches receiving a second pastor had experienced significant conflict** in the church (where either people left the church or a special meeting had to be held to deal with the conflict) in the year before the pastoral change.

By the time second pastors arrive, churches tend to be worshiping in their own space (68 percent) rather than in rented space. Whatever their worship meeting place, congregations on average have been worshiping in that same space for 3 years. But just over 20 percent of churches receiving a second pastor have been in their current worship space one year or less.

Virtually all of the second pastors said they were good or very good in making sure systems are in place and working well—such as systems for outreach, hospitality, incorporation of new people, worship, etc. That is fortunate since 70 percent report that such 4 systems were only adequate or were poor to nonexistent when they arrived. This may be a combination of second pastors having a different set of skills from what it takes to start a church and the tendency to judge ourselves a bit less harshly than we do our predecessors.

To what extent does the appointment of a second pastor lead to staff conflict or turnover? Surely that happens, but not so much as might be expected. By and large, **over three-fourths of people on staff when the** second pastor arrived (clergy and lay, full and part time) were still on staff one year later. And when there were staff transitions in the first year, over 60 percent report those changes going smoothly or relatively smoothly. But in almost 40 percent of the cases where there was staff change (although not involving many staff), the transitions were reported as somewhat or very contentious.

Second pastors give most of their time in the first year to worship and sermon preparation, leadership development, getting to know people, and evangelism.

When comparing second pastors and founding pastors, male second pastors tend to follow male founding pastors in 80 percent of the cases studied. But about 10 percent have male second pastors following female founding pastors or female second pastors following male founding pastors. Appointments in recent years indicate that future surveys will show more diverse patterns.

When asked how similar or different they are from their predecessors in personality, approach to ministry, theology, and priorities, 75 percent of second pastors said they are somewhat or very different from their predecessor. Despite these differences, second pastors overwhelmingly describe their relationship with the founding pastor as very good or cordial and professional.

Advice from second pastors to new second pastors about relating to the founding pastor focused on: ask and listen, respect what they have done, affirm them, and never criticize them. Every congregation has a personality or DNA. When asked how closely their personal characteristics matched the culture of the congregations where they were sent, 65 percent of second pastors reported their characteristics were similar to the culture of the congregation, with the largest response being very similar.

When asked about similarities or differences upon arrival with the predominant population the church was seeking to reach (age, race, education, family, background), over 70 percent of second pastors said they were similar to the population the church is seeking to reach, with the largest response being very similar.

According to those surveyed, the characteristics needed by second pastors are patience, self-confidence, listener, thick skin, vision, and flexibility.

The second pastors surveyed said there will always be comparisons to the founder so take them in stride and keep moving forward. Realize that you are not the founding pastor, and your credibility will take time to establish. Build on your strengths, and focus on public moments when you make first impressions. Make sure your preaching is passionate and creative and be yourself.

When asked what new second pastors should and should not do when they begin as second pastors, those surveyed said second pastors should listen; affirm the founding pastor; get to know the leaders, staff, and members; and understand the history and DNA of the congregation. They caution against changing things quickly and criticizing the founding pastor.

What Matters Most to Growth in Attendance

The Lewis Center engaged Donald R. House, PhD, to do an analysis of survey results in relationship to worship attendance trends before and after the arrival of the second pastor to see if there were statistically significant factors that help or hinder attendance growth during the second pastor's tenure.

The longer the founding pastor stayed, the greater the attendance reported by the second pastor. This is not surprising if attendance continues to grow during the years of the founding pastor. Great attendance before the arrival of the second pastor merely places the second pastor on a higher plane.

Attendance is greater the older the second pastor—up to age 42. After age 42, attendance declines. Since earlier research has shown attendance growth in new church starts associated with young clergy (under 35 when they begin), this may mean that a greater degree of experience and maturity may be needed to face the challenges of being a second pastor, including following a charismatic, maybe younger, founding pastor.

Attendance grows with time during the tenure of the second pastor. As expected, it grows at a decreasing rate. Our data stop at 13 years in the appointment, and over the range of 1 to 13 years, it never turns downward, but it begins to flatten somewhat.

Interestingly, the second pastor's attendance is greater if there was a conflict in the church toward the end of the founding pastor's tenure. Perhaps this makes it easier for the church to welcome the second pastor.

Attendance for the second pastor is greater if the two pastors are more similar. Perhaps the founding pastor attracted a congregation with an affinity for the founding pastor's characteristics. If the second pastor has similar characteristics, the congregation seems to respond positively.

The second pastor's attendance is greater if the second pastor better matches the church's DNA—perhaps not surprising at all. We did not find a significant relationship between the second pastor's attendance and similarity between the second pastor and the people the church is trying to reach. We believe the wording of this question may have been somewhat confusing, thus skewing the results.

Possible Implications for Selecting Second Pastors

Do not look for transitional pastors unless extraordinary circumstances call for that. Recognize that the second pastor is going to be there for a while, and the church will continue to grow.

Look for someone a bit older than most new church planters, but not too old. An age in the range of 38 to 42 seems to be ideal.

The second pastor needs demonstrated emotional and professional maturity with self-confidence and a clarity of call. The second pastor will need utmost patience. Avoid negative personalities and those who make a habit of criticizing their predecessors.

The skills needed for the second pastor are similar to and different from those needed by the founding pastor. Both require energy, vision, and a passion for people experiencing new life in Christ. Second pastors need to be good at ensuring that ministry systems are in place and are built around teams and not just the pastor.

There is always a debate about whether the second pastor should be similar to or different from the founding pastor. Most second pastors feel they are different from their predecessors, but attendance grows better the more similar the pastors are. Perhaps the second pastor needs to be somewhat different but not radically different. However, sending a second pastor whose approach to ministry is in sync with the culture of the new congregation is essential.

Be careful not to make the change too soon. The presence of significant conflict in 60 percent of churches in the year before the founding pastor left may indicate that the time for the change of pastors was right. Since the conflict did not hamper the church's attendance growth once the second pastor arrived (actually helped), one conclusion may be that those without the conflict may have done better with the founding pastor staying a bit longer.

If there are other ordained staff at the church, there is no need to think that the other clergy must move when the founding pastor moves. Most second pastors work well with inherited staff. However, if there is strong reason to believe that the clergy staff will not be supportive of the new pastor, then that is a different situation. While there is not much staff transition in the first year, when it does occur, often it does not go well.

Reprinted with permission from the Lewis Center for Church Leadership of Wesley Theological Seminary, Washington, DC, www.churchleadership.com.

"Why We Joined" Form

Why We (I) Joined

Thank you for your recent decision to join _____
Church. We are very pleased that you chose to become part of this community of faith and look forward to great days ahead.

We want to provide the very best ministry possible. Please complete this brief questionnaire and return it in the pre-addressed envelope. This important information helps us greatly. *Thanks!*

1. How would you rate the following?

	Completely Satisfied	Very Satisfied	Satisfied	Somewhat Satisfied	Very Dissatisfied
Overall Church Facilities					
Design of Church					
Parking					
Restrooms					
"Feel" of Worship Service					
Sanctuary					
Social Media					

Music					
Graphics					
Sermon					
Outreach & Missions					
Nursery Care					
Nursery Facilities					
Sunday School Rooms					
Sunday School & Small Group Program					
Youth Program					
Children's Program					

2. Please circle the appropriate answer:

    a.   Did the staff members greet you and treat you courteously? Yes No

    b.   Did church members greet you and treat you courteously? Yes No

    c.   Have you been contacted by anyone in the church since you joined? Yes No

3. Please share about your decision to join _____.

    a. What influenced you to visit here?

    b. Did you visit other churches? If so, where?

    c. What or who impressed you about the church?

    d. If you visited other churches, what was the main reason you chose not to join there?

4. Please rank the top 10 of the following (10 being the most important and 1 being the least) in your decision to join:

___Time of Service
___Theology
___Worship Services
___Special Groups
___Location of Church
___Size of Church
___Friendliness of Congregation
___Reputation of Church
___Biblical Interpretation
___Denominational Importance
___Met My Needs
___Activities and Programs
___Sunday School
___Opportunities for Involvement and Service
___Other:

5. What is most positive about this church for you?

6. What would you like to see changed or improved?

Notes

Introduction

1. Lovett Weems, "It Is Not Enough to Be Right," *Faith and Leadership*, Oct. 10, 2011, www.faithandleadership.com/qa/lovett-h-weems-it-not-enough-be-right.

3. The Role of Supervisors

1. Michael D. Watkins, *The First 90 Days: Proven Strategies for Getting Up to Speed Faster and Smarter* (Boston: Harvard Business Review Press, 2013), 69–82.

5. The Role of the Departing Pastor

1. Robert Kaylor, *Your Best Move* (Wilmore, KY: Seedbed Press, 2013), 15.

2. Ibid., 67ff.

6. The Role of the Incoming Pastor

1. "Fanny Blankers-Koen, Star of '48 Olympics, Dies at 85," *New York Times*, Jan. 26, 2004.

2. Jim Collins, *Good to Great: Why Some Companies Make the Leap . . . and Others Don't* (New York: HarperBusiness, 2001), 52–55.

3. http://www.fastcompany.com/3044962/hit-the-ground-running/3-counterintuitive-things-you-should-do-after-you-get-a-promotion.

7. Creating a Culture of Accountability

1.   https://en.wikipedia.org/wiki/Athletics_at_the_2012_Summer_Olympics_–_Men%27s_4_x_400_metres_relay#cite_note-4.

2. Patrick Lencioni, *The Advantage: Why Organizational Health Trumps Everything Else in Business* (San Francisco: Josey-Bass, 2012), 144–72.

3. Tom Mullins, *Passing the Leadership Baton* (Nashville: Thomas Nelson, 2015), 67.

4. Watkins, *First 90 Days*, 240–42.

12. What to Expect in the Changeover Zone

1. General Stanley McChrystal, *Team of Teams: New Rules of Engagement for a Complex World* (New York: Portfolio/Penguin, 2015), 222.

2. Ibid., 225.

3. Ibid., 229.

Epilogue

1. Joel Greenberg, *A Feathered River Across the Sky: The Passenger Pigeon's Flight to Extinction* (New York: Bloomsbury, 2014).

2. A frequently stated sentiment, most recently attributed to Lord Carey, Archbishop of Canterbury. Leonardo Blair, "Christianity Is 'a Generation Away From Extinction' in Britain, Says Former Archbishop of Canterbury," *Christian Post*, Nov. 20, 2013, http://www.christianpost.com/news/christianity-is-a-generation-away-from-extinction-in-britain-says-former-archbishop-of-canterbury-109184.

Made in the USA
Lexington, KY
25 March 2019